Table of Contents

Preparation and Professional Issues

Learning Objectives

- Identify levels of EMS training.

- Identify key federal legislation related to EMS.

- List the various medical, legal, and ethical issues related to emergency care.

- Understands each body system and the medical terminology.

- Identifies the various ways to lift and move patients.

The modern EMS system originated from funeral homes, which used to operate ambulances. In the best interest of the patient, the EMS profession evolved, and now serves the larger public health system through prevention efforts and public education. Some of the milestones related to EMS include:

- 1980s – The American Heart Association (AHA) increased awareness of cardiovascular disease prevention, and additional EMS levels of training were added to accommodate this.

- 1990s – The National Registry of Emergency Medical Technicians (NREMT) advocated national training for EMS providers, and the National Highway Transportation Safety Administration (NHTSA) started the *EMS Agenda for the Future* document.

- 2000s – The NHTSA replaces standard curricula with the National EMS Education Standards (NEMSES), and four levels of licensure and certification were created.

Introduction to Emergency Medical Care

Levels of Training

- Emergency Medical Responder (EMR) - These persons provide basic and immediate care to patients who have issues with bleeding, require CPR or AED, and for women who having emergency childbirth.

- Emergency Medical Technician (EMT) - These people are EMR providers who have additional skills in ventilation and oxygenation, pulse oximetry, vital sign monitoring, and administration of certain medications.

- Advanced Emergency Medical Technician (AEMT) - These individuals possess all EMT skills, as well as intravenous and intraosseous access, advanced airway devices, blood glucose monitoring, and administration of additional medications.

- Paramedic - This is the top level of advanced EMT, in which these people have management skills and advanced assessment abilities. This includes extensive pharmacology interventions, invasive skills, and the highest level of pre-hospital care allowed under the National EMS Education Standards.

A medical assistant must maintain a professional attitude and appearance at all times. The healthcare environment can be both stressful and humorous, but it is always best to maintain a sense of professionalism. This section covers professional attitude, job readiness, seeking employment, and working as a team member.

Professional Attitude

A professional attitude involves appropriate communication with patients, physicians, and other healthcare workers. Good communication skills include refraining from slang, jargon or phrases that are unfamiliar to patients and other healthcare workers. Speaking in a well-educated manner is crucial in order to portray a professional image of yourself and the facility where you work. It is a must that an EMT-B is proficient in both written and spoken grammar.

Qualities of a Good Employee

After securing a position, the medical assistant must always look and do his or her best. An employer expects the employee to perform with increasing expertise as he or she gains experience. Certain qualities are significantly important for holding a job. The desirable employee qualities that employers usually rank as most important are:

- Communication skills
- Dependability
- Cooperation
- Courteousness
- Enthusiasm
- Initiative
- Interest

- Punctuality
- Math skills
- Reading skills
- Time management skills
- Reliability
- Responsibility

Medical, Legal, and Ethical Issues

Ethics are principles of conduct that govern a person or group. The National Association of Emergency Medical Technicians (NAEMT) adopted the EMT Code of Ethics in 1978, and this allows professions in this filed to have standards of ethics to adhere. As an EMT-Basic provider, the professional pledges to follow this code of professional ethics with a fundamental responsibility to preserve life, alleviate suffer, promote health, encourage quality, do no harm and provide emergency medical care.

Ethical Responsibilities

- Practice and maintain skills at the master level.

- Make the patient's needs a priority, both physical and emotional

- Critically review performance, by responding to patient outcomes, providing communication reviewing performances, and seeking ways to improve response time.

- Attend continuing education courses and programs.

- Report things in an honest manner.

Medical Supervision

EMS providers operate under the license of a physician medical director. The EMT-B should always contact the medical director when he or she is unsure of how to

manage a patient. It is necessary for EMTs to know the guidelines, standards, and protocols of the state, agency, and of the medical director.

Scope of Practice

The scope of practice for the EMT-B outlines the actions the provider should legally perform based on certification level. The scope of practice is associated with licensure or certification status, not the person's experience, skill level, or knowledge base. Each state can determine the scope of practice for the EMS provider, and the National EMS Education Standards (NEMSES) aligns this scope throughout the United States.

Standards of Care

A care standard is the degree of care a person is responsible for with a certain level of training when compared to someone with the exact same training who is performing the exact same task or skill. Standard of care involves the "reasonable person test," which is a question asking: What would a reasonable person with the same training do in this same situation? These standards require the EMT-Basic to perform an indicated assessment and treatment within his or her scope of practice.

Sources that Establish Standards of Care

- Medical Director

- National EMS Education Standards

- State Protocols and Guidelines

- EMS Agency Policies and Procedures

- EMT Reputable Textbooks

- Community Standards for EMTs

Advanced Directives

The EMT-Basic has the responsibility to honor a patient's preferences in providing quality of life care, especially when end-of-life is considered. To assist physicians and other healthcare providers, this involves conveying a patient's wishes regarding CPR and other life-sustaining treatments.

- Do Not Resuscitate (DNR) - The DNR order is specific to which resuscitation efforts are allowed, and it does not apply to treatment that occurs before cardiac arrest.

- Living will - The living will addresses wishes before the patient has cardiac arrest. This may include feeding tubes, advanced airways, and other measures.

Out-of-Hospital DNR Orders

- Require written order from the physician.

- Patient has the right to deny or refuse any efforts for resuscitation.

- EMT-B should review the DNR order.

- EMT-B should understand state and local legislation and protocols relative to advanced directives.

Forms of Consent

- *Implied consent* - This is consent assumed from the unconscious patient who requires emergency intervention. Implied consent is based on the assumption that the patient needs life-saving interventions.
- *Express consent* - The patient must be able to make rational decisions, be of legal age, and be informed of all steps of the procedures, as well as procedural risks. With expressed consent, the patient is conscious and mentally competent to render treatment.
- *Consent for children and mentally incompetent people* - For children and adults who are mentally disabled, the EMT-B must obtain consent from a parent or legal guardian. When a life-threatening issue arises, the consent for emergency treatment is rendered based on implied consent.
- *Emancipation* - With emancipation issues, a patient legally under age should be recognized as having the legal capacity to give consent. Emancipated persons have criteria based on set regulations that vary state to state. Emancipated minors are those who are pregnant or married, people who are already a parent, members of the armed forces, persons emancipated by the courts, and those who are financially independent.

Liability of the EMT-B

Good Samaritan Laws

Various Good Samaritan laws protect people who render care as long as that person is not grossly negligent and is not being compensated. Each state has some form of these laws.

- *Criminal liability* - Assault is when a person is found guilty of harming another person by inflicting physical harm. However, physical contact is not always

9

necessary for assault to apply. Battery is when a person physically touches another person without his or her consent.

- *Civil liability* - With civil law, a person can sue another for wrongful act that results in some form of damage. Some civil suits involve just one EMS provider, but others involve all providers, as well as the medical director and supervisor of the EMS unit.

- *Negligence* - With negligence, the EMS provider is accused of some form of unintentional harm that occurs to a patient. This involves:

  - *Duty to act* - The EMT-B has the obligation to respond and provide care.

  - *Breach of duty* - The EMT has failed to assess and treat the patient by standard care measures.

  - *Damage* - The patient experiences some form of injury due recognized in the legal system as worthy of compensation.

  - *Causation* - Called proximate cause, this is an injury to a patient that was directly related to the EMT-B's breach of duty.

- *Abandonment* - Once an EMS provider begins rendering patient care, he or she cannot terminate care without the patient's consent. Most agencies have written protocols regarding terminating care without transporting the patient to a higher level of care.

Patient Refusals

Refusal for treatment often occurs on emergency call outs. The competent patient may refuse treatment regardless of his or her condition. The refusal can present liability for the EMT-B, especially regarding abandonment and negligence issues. If this occurs, make attempts to contact the supervisor or medical director. To refuse treatment, the patient should be:

- Aware of his or her circumstances

- Aware of person, place, and time

- Of legal age

- Mentally competent

Documenting Refusals

If a patient refuses, the EMT must properly document the refusal after exhausting the following measures:

- Make several attempts to persuade the patient to receive care or go to the hospital.

- Consider assistance by law enforcement.

- Assure that he or she is able to make an informed, rational decision.

- Ensure that the patient is not under the influence of drugs or alcohol.

- Inform the patient of the circumstances or issues that could occur if he or she does not get treatment.

- Consult the supervisor or medical director.

- Document assessment findings and any emergency care that was given.

- Fill out a refusal form, and make sure the patient signs that form.

Duty to Act

- *Implied* - A duty to act where the patient calls 911/EMS and the dispatcher confirms that help is on the way.

- *Formal* - The EMS has a written contract with a municipality. Such clauses within the contract should indicate which service may be refused by the patient.

- *Legal* - While legal duty to act may not exist, there is a moral and ethical consideration.

- *State-specific* - In some states, when an EMT comes upon an accident, he or she must provide assistance.

Health Insurance Portability and Accountability Act

There are numerous requirements relative to the Health and Insurance Portability Act (HIPAA) for EMS providers. These include:

- Any covered provider should give a patient a notice of their rights and responsibilities related to privacy, but the provider does not need to obtain prior consent that would affect access to care.

11

- The patient should give permission in advance in a form of disclosure, and one form can be used for all aspects of the privacy policies.

- A covered entity must get written authorization to use health information for marketing purposes.

- A covered entity should account for disclosures of protected health information in the six years prior to the person's request.

- A patent may request restriction of use and disclosure of protected health information.

Releasing Confidential Information

Confidential information requires a signed written release to be sent or released. The EMS providers cannot release on request unless legal guardianship has been established or the patient specifically requests for this process. Certain state laws require reporting incidents, such as abuse or rape, and releasing information does not require consent in these incidents.

The EMS agency must implement policies and procedures to comply with HIPAA, written communication, document all procedures, policies, and required actions, and maintain documentation for six years. Also the services should education and train employees, provider a complaint process, mitigate the harmful effects of improper disclosure, and apply workforce sanctions for violations.

When releasing confidential information, the EMS agency should use a written release form that has to be signed by the patient. Do not release on request unless legal guardianship is known and established. Also, when a release form is necessary, other healthcare providers involved should be informed of this to continue the patient's care. State laws regarding reporting abuse, rape, and assault vary.

Working as a Team Member

In addition to physicians and other EMS providers, the EMT-B will work with a variety of healthcare team members. Each person performs a specific set of duties for which he or she is trained. Many of these team members have direct contact with the medical assistant. It is necessary to be knowledgeable about the various allied health professionals, such as:

- *Admissions Clerk* – An admissions clerk in a medical office has basic administrative office skills. He or she obtains basic medical history and information from patient when they come into the facility.

- *Certified Nursing Assistant (CNA)* – A CNA provides basic nursing skills and patient care to people in adult day care centers, nursing homes, office settings, and hospitals. This person is registered and/or licensed.

- *Emergency Medical Technician (EMT)* – An EMT is a person trained in the administration of emergency care and transportation of patients to the medical facility.

- *Laboratory Technician* – Often called a medical technologist, a laboratory technician is someone who works under the supervision of a pathologist or physician. These healthcare workers perform chemical, microscopic, and/or bacteriologic testing on blood and body tissues.

- *Licensed Practical Nurse (LPN)* – An LPN is a one-year nurse who is trained in patient care and licensed by the state.

- *Registered Nurse (RN)* – An RN is a two- or four-year nurse who is trained in patient care and licensed by the state.

- *Nurse Practitioner (NP)* – An NP is a RN who has advanced training to diagnose and treat patients in the healthcare environment.

- *Phlebotomist* – Also called an accessioning technician, a phlebotomist is a person who is trained in drawing blood.

- *Physician Assistant (PA)* – A PA is a person trained to practice medicine under the supervision of a physician.

- *Radiologic Technologist (RT)* – Also called an x-ray technician, an RT is a person who is trained to operate radiologic equipment under the supervision of a physician.

Communication

The care of patients involves many different individuals and all types of healthcare providers. Therefore, it is necessary for there to be effective and meaningful communication for healthcare delivery. Communication systems are formal and informal structures used to support the communication needs within an organization. Elements of these systems are the communication channel, type of message, policies, agent, services, device, interaction mode, and security protocol. Also, effective communication relies on useful style and principles of sharing information, negotiation concepts and strategies, and communication processes that support safe patient care.

Anatomical Terminology

- *Anatomical plane* - A surface where any two points are taken. To find this, a straight line is drawn to join these two points, within that surface of plane.
- *Normal anatomical position* - A person facing forward with palms facing forward.
- *Midline* - An imaginary line drawn vertically through the middle region of the body, such as nose to umbilicus.
- *Midaxillary* - An imaginary line drawn vertically from the middle of the armpit to the ankle, dividing the body into anterior and posterior.
- *Torso* - Body trunk
- *Midclavicular* - Line in the center of the clavicle
- *Bilateral* - Both sides
- *Dorsal* - Toward the back
- *Ventral* - Toward front
- *Prone* - Face down
- *Supine* - Face up
- *Plantar* - Of the sole of the foot
- *Palmar* - Of the palm
- *Fowler's position* - Sitting at a 90 degree angle
- *Trendelenburg* position - Lying supine with lower body elevated
- *Shock position* - Body supine with legs elevated 8 to 12 inches

Directional Terms

- *Superior* - Toward the head, or toward the upper body region.
- *Inferior* - Toward the lower part of the body.
- *Anterior (Ventral)* - On the belly or front side of the body.

- *Posterior (Dorsal)* - On the buttocks or back side of the body.

- *Proximal* - Near the trunk or middle part of the body.

- *Distal* - Furthest away from the point of reference.

- *Medial* - Close to the midline of the body.

- *Lateral* - Away from the midline of the body.

Respiratory System

Moves oxygen through the body and eliminates carbon dioxide from the body.

Terminology

- *Apnea* - When breathing stops.

- *Asphyxia* - Lack of oxygen.

- *Atelectasis* - Incomplete lung expansion.

- *Auscultation* - Listening to lung sounds.

- *Bronchiole* - Small division of the bronchial tree.

- *Cyanosis* - Bluish discoloration of the skin or lips.

- *Dyspnea* - Shortness of breath.

- *Epistaxis* - Nose bleed.

- *Hemoptysis* - Coughing up blood.

- *Hypoxia* - Reduced oxygenation of the tissue.

- *Intubation* - Insertion of a tube.

- *Lavage* - Washing out.

- *Orthopnea* - Shortness of breath with lying.

- *Pleura* - Lining that covers the lungs.

- *Pleuritis* - Inflammation of the pleura.

- *Rhinorrhea* - Drainage from the nose.

- *Tachypnea* - Rapid respiratory rate.

Human Respiratory System

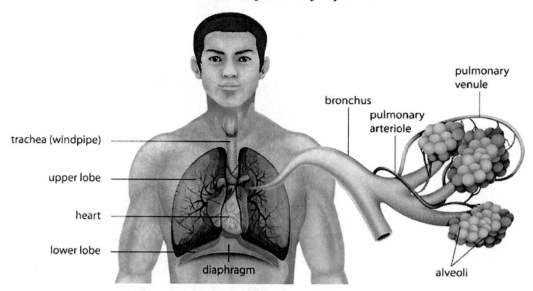

Respiratory Assessment

- *Rhythm*: Regular or irregular

- *Breath sounds*: Present and equal vs. diminished or absent

- *Chest expansion*: Adequate and equal vs. unequal and inadequate

- *Effort of breathing*: No use vs. use of accessory muscles

Upper Airway

- *Nose and mouth*

- *Nasopharynx* (upper part of the throat behind the nose)

- *Oropharynx* (area of the throat behind the mouth)

- *Larynx* (voice box)

- *Epiglottis* (valve that protects the trachea opening)

Lower Airway

- *Trachea* (windpipe)

- *Carina* (area where trachea branches into bronchi)

- *Bronchi* (right and left primary branches of the trachea leading to lungs)

- *Bronchioles* (small branches of bronchi)

- *Alveoli* (small airway structures that diffuse oxygen from the respiratory system)

- *Breathing Muscles and Lung Expansion*

- *Pleura* - Two smooth layers of lung tissue that allow frictionless movement across one another.

- *Diaphragm* - Primary muscle of respiration that separates the thoracic cavity and is under involuntary control, for the most part.

- *Intercostal muscles* - Structures between the ribs that contract during inhalation and expand the thoracic cage.

Circulatory System

Also called the cardiovascular system, this system circulates blood through the body.

Blood Flow in Human Circulatory System

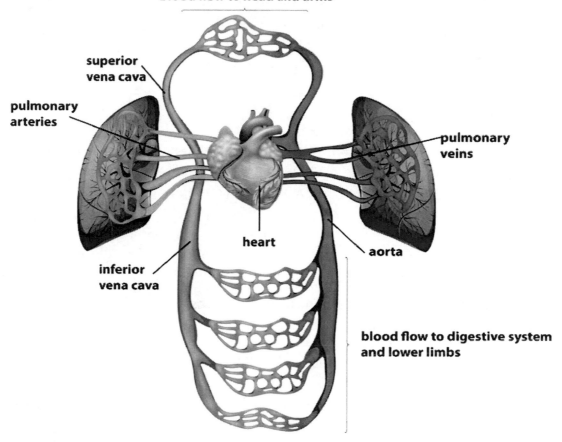

Terminology

- *Aneurysm* - Abnormal dilation of artery.

- *Angina* - Chest pain described as spasmodic and choking.

- *Angiography* - Diagnostic test on the blood vessels.

- *Angioplasty* - Procedure used to dilate a vessel opening.

- *Bundle of His* - Cardiac fibers that allow heart rhythm.

- *Circumflex* - A coronary artery that encircles the heart.

- *Edema* - Swelling due to fluid collection in the tissue.

- *Electrophysiology* - The study of the heart's electrical system.

- *Embolectomy* - Removal of an embolism or blockage from a vessel.

- *Epicardial* - Over the heart.

- *Fistula* - Opening from one area to the other or to the outside of the body.

- *Hemolysis* - RBC breakdown.

- *Intracardiac* - Inside the heart.

- *Thoracostomy* - Incisions made into the chest wall to insert a chest tube.

- *Transvenous* - Through a vein.

Heart

The heart is a muscular organ that has two pumps, the left and right ventricles. The left ventricle receives oxygenated blood from the lungs and sends it throughout the body. The right pump receives oxygen-poor blood, and sends it to the lungs.

Blood

- *Function* - To maintain a constant environment, carry oxygen and nutrients to cells, delivery waste and carbon dioxide to organs, and transport hormones from the endocrine system.

- *Liquid part* - Plasma is extracellular with 91% water.

- *Cellular part* - Contains leukocytes (white blood cells WBCs), erythrocytes (red blood cells or RBCs), and thrombocytes (platelets).

Vessels

- *Function* - To transport blood and carry away cellular waste and carbon dioxide.

- *Arteries* - Lead away from the heart and branch into arterioles.

- *Veins* - Lead to the heart and branch into venules.

- *Capillaries* - Connect between arterioles and venules

Heart Muscle Layers

- *Endocardium* - Smooth lining inside the heart.

- *Myocardium* - Thick muscular heart wall.

- *Epicardium* - Outer layer of the heart and inner layer of pericardium.

- *Pericardium* - Fibrous sac around the heart.

Heart Chambers and Valves

- *Atria* - The two upper heart chambers. The atria pumps blood into the ventricles right before they contract, which is called an "atrial kick."

- *Ventricles* - The lower heart chambers that receive blood from the atria and send it throughout the body during ventricular contraction. Ventricular contraction generates a palpable pulse.

- Heart valves - One-way valves that are between the atria and ventricles, which allow blood to move in a downward direction into the ventricles during atrial contraction.

Conduction System

The heart has a conduction (electrical) system, which generates electrical impulses and stimulates heart muscle contraction. The primary area is the sinoatrial (SA) node, which generates anywhere from 60 to 100 impulses per minute in the adult. The backup pacemaker is the atrioventricular (AV) junction, which generates electrical impulses at around 40 to 60 per minute. The Bundle of His is a pacemaker that can generate around 20 to 40 impulses per minute.

Cardiac Contraction

- *Myocardial contractility* - The ability of the heart to contract, which requires adequate blood volume and muscle strength.

- *Preload* - The pre-contraction pressure based on the amount of blood that flows back to the heart. An increased preload leads to increased ventricular stretching of the ventricles and increased contractility.

- *Afterload* - The resistance which the heart must overcome during contraction of the ventricles. If there is an increase in afterload, there is decreased cardiac output.

Blood Flow

Blood flows through the cardiovascular system in a complex method. Oxygen-rick blood leaves the heart via the aorta, which branches off into arteries, then arterioles, and then capillaries. The capillaries feed into the venules, to the veins, and then into the superior or inferior vena cava.

Arteries carry blood away from the heart and veins carry blood to the heart. The pulmonary artery carries deoxygenated blood, where the pulmonary vein carries oxygen-rich blood.

The Path of Blood Flow

- The vena cava returns blood to the right atrium.

- The right atrium pumps blood into the right ventricle.

- The right ventricle pumps oxygen-poor blood to the pulmonary arteries and then to the lungs.

- Carbon dioxide and oxygen exchange occurs between the alveoli and capillaries.

- The lungs send oxygen-rich blood to the heart via the pulmonary veins.

- Blood enters the left atrium which pumps blood to the left ventricle.

- From the left ventricle, the blood enters the aorta for circulation throughout the body.

Systemic Vascular Resistance (SVR)

Systemic vascular resistance (SVR) is a resistance to blood flow in the body, but this excludes the pulmonary system. SVR is related to blood vessel size:

- *Constriction* - This is reduced size, which increases SVR and blood pressure.

- *Dilation* - This is increased size, which lowers SVR and blood pressure.

Components of the Blood

- *Plasma* - Liquid that is mostly water.

- *Platelets* - Necessary for clot formation to stop bleeding.

- *Red blood cells (RBCs)* - Also called erythrocytes, these cells carry oxygen.

- *White blood cells (WBCs)* - Also called leukocytes, these cells fight infection.

Blood Pressure

Blood pressure (BP) is a measurement of pressure exerted against the artery walls. The systolic pressure is when the blood pressure exerts during contraction of the left ventricle, and diastolic pressure is the pressure between contractions.

Blood Perfusion

Blood perfusion is the flow of blood through the body. When there is adequate perfusion, the organs and tissues receive oxygen-rich blood. However, with inadequate perfusion, also called shock, the blood flow is compromised.

Musculoskeletal System

Provides shape, protects the internal organs, and allows body movement.

The musculoskeletal system is comprised of the bony skeleton, skeletal muscles, cardiac muscles, and smooth muscles. There also are 206 bones, as well as cartilage and ligaments. The muscular system protects the organs, produces heat, assists with movement, and forms body shape.

Components of the Skeletal System

- *Bones* - 206 in the human body

- *Ligaments* - Connect bone to bone.

- *Tendons* - Connect bone to muscle.

- *Cartilage* - Connective tissue that allows joint movement.

Types of Bones

- *Long Bones* - Tubular (femur, tibia, fibula, humerus, ulna, and radius)

- *Short Bones* - Cuboidal (carpals and tarsals)

- *Flat Bones* - Thin and flat (scapula, sternum, and skull)

- *Irregular Bones* - Varied shapes (zygoma and vertebrae)

- *Sesamoid* - Rounded (patella)

Axial Skeleton

The skull, spinal column, and rib cage make up the axial skeleton.

- *Facial Bones* - maxilla (upper jaw), nasal (bridge of nose), zygomatic (cheekbone), mandible (jaw), lacrimal (near eye orbits), vomer (nasal septum), palate (between oral and nasal cavities), and nasal conchae (turbinates).

- *Hyoid Bone* - U-shaped bone that supports the tongue.

- *Spine* - 33 vertebrae (7 cranial, 12 thoracic, 5 lumbar, 5 sacrum, and 4 coccyx).

- *Thorax Bones* - 12 pairs of ribs and the sternum.

Skull Bones

- *Frontal* - Forehead bone
- *Parietal* - Bone on top of the head
- *Occipital* - Bone in the back of the skull
- *Temporal* - Lateral bones above the cheekbones

- *Maxillae* - Bones that form the upper jaw

- *Mandible* - The moveable portion of the lower jaw

- *Zygomatic* - The cheekbones

- *Nasal* - The bone of the nose

- *Foramen magnum* - The opening in the occipital bone that connects brain to spinal cord.

HUMAN SKULL side view

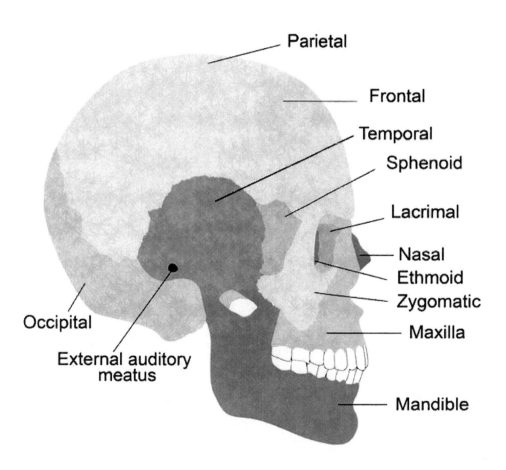

Spinal Column Components

- *Vertebrae* - 33 vertebrae form the spine.

- *Cervical vertebrae* - C1 to C7

- *Thoracic vertebrae* - T1 to T12

- *Lumbar vertebrae* - L1 to L5

- *Sacrum* - 5 fused vertebrae

- *Coccyx* - 4 fused vertebrae

Thoracic Cavity

- *Sternum* - Breast bone

- *Manubrium* - Upper sternum

- *Body* - Middle section of the sternum

- *Xiphoid process* - The inferior tip of the sternum

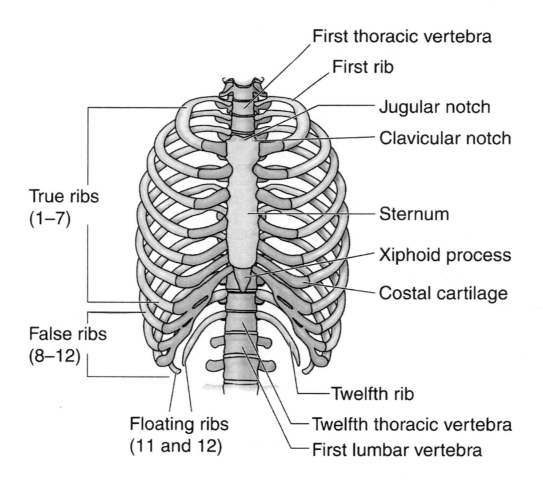

First thoracic vertebra

First rib

Jugular notch

Clavicular notch

True ribs (1–7)

Sternum

Xiphoid process

Costal cartilage

False ribs (8–12)

Twelfth rib

Floating ribs (11 and 12)

Twelfth thoracic vertebra

First lumbar vertebra

Appendicular Skeleton

The appendicular skeleton includes the bones of the legs, arms, and pelvis. These include:

- *Clavicle* - Collarbone

- *Scapula* - Shoulder blade

- *Humerus* - Upper arm

- *Radius* - Lateral forearm bone

- *Ulna* - Medial forearm bone

- *Carpals* - Wrist bones

- *Metacarpals* - Base of the fingers

- *Phalanges* - Fingers

- *Ilium* - Upper area of pelvis

- *Ischium* - Lower area of pelvis

- *Pubis* - Anterior portion of pelvis

- *Femur* - Thigh bone

- *Patella* - Kneecap

- *Tibia* - Medial lower leg bone

- *Fibula* - Lateral lower leg bone

- *Tarsals* - Ankle bones

- *Metatarsals* - Base of toes

- *Phalanges* - Toes

Joints

A joint is where two bones come together. The three types of joints are:

- *Hinge joint* - Where bones can move in only one direction (knee).

- *Ball-and-socket joint* - Where distal ends of bones have free motion (shoulder).

- *Symphysis joint* - Limited movement.

Muscles

There are three types of muscles. These include:

- *Cardiac* - Heart muscle

- *Smooth* - Involuntary muscle (blood vessels and digestive tract)

- *Skeletal* - Voluntary muscle attaches to the skeleton, which includes:
    - *Biceps* - Anterior humerus
    - *Triceps* - Posterior humerus
    - *Pectoralis* - Anterior chest
    - *Latissimus dorsi* - Posterior chest
    - *Rectus abdominis* - Abdominal muscles

- ○ *Quadriceps* - Anterior femur
- ○ *Gluteus* – Buttocks

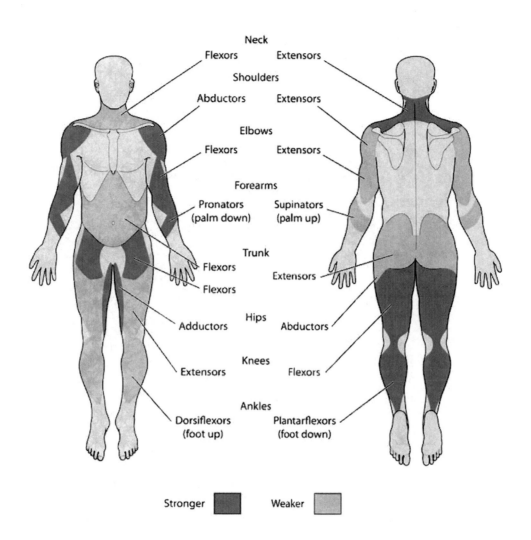

Central Nervous System

The central nervous system (CNS) includes the brain and spinal cord. This is the command center for the body. The brain receives information and makes decisions. After that, the brain tells the peripheral nervous system (PNS) what to do. The nervous system controls, regulates, and communicates with the various structures, organs, and body parts.

CNS Components

- *Cerebrum* - Controls memory, thought, and senses.

- *Cerebellum* - Coordinates movement, balance, and fine motor ability.

- *Brain stem* - Controls breathing and consciousness.

- *Cerebrospinal fluid (CSF)* - Clear fluid of the brain and spinal cord that filters contaminants and cushions the CNS.

Neurons

The primary cells of the nervous system. There are four types:

- *Dendrites* (receive nerve signals)

- *Cell body* (nucleus)

- *Axon* (carries nerve signals)

- *Mylein sheath* (around the axon).

Brain

- *Brainstem* – Consists of the medulla oblongata, pons, and midbrain.

- *Diencephalon* – Consists of the hypothalamus and thalamus.

- *Cerebellum* – Structure that controls voluntary movement and balance.

- *Cerebrum* – Large portion of the brain.

- *Lobes:* Frontal, parietal, temporal, occipital, and insula.

Nerves

Cranial – 12 pair
Spinal – 31 pair

Peripheral Nervous System

The peripheral nervous system includes the structures outside the CNS, such as the nerves. This system sends information to the CNS, and delivers instructions from the CNS. The two divisions of the PNS are:

- *Sensory division* - Sends information to the CNS.

- *Motor division* – Receive commands from the CNS.

Autonomic Nervous System

The autonomic nervous system (ANS) is the involuntary portion of the PNS. The two portions of this system are:

- *Sympathetic* - "Fight or flight" which works in times of stress.

- *Parasympathetic* - "Feed and breed" which controls rest, reproduction, and digestion.

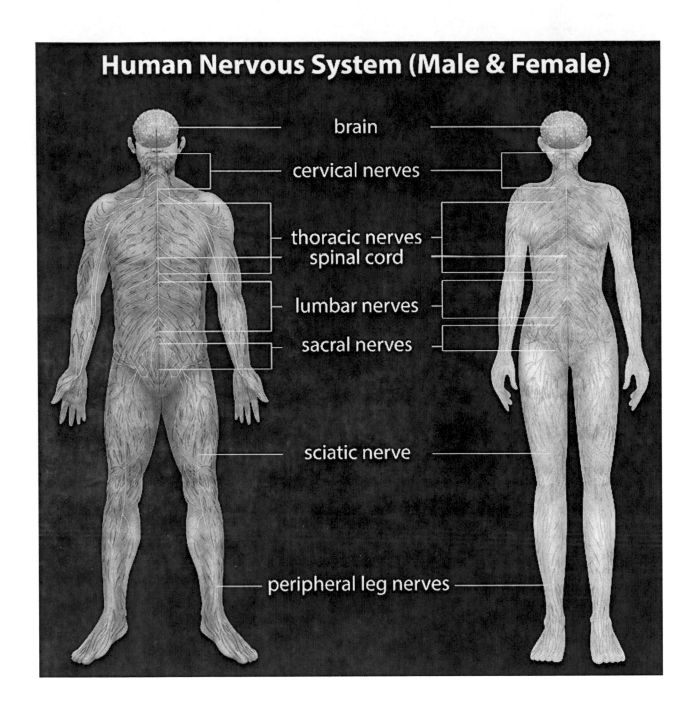

Integumentary System

The integument is the skin, which makes up around 18% of the body's weight. Skin is necessary to protect a person from the invasion of microorganisms, as well as to regulate body temperature and manufacture vitamins. The skin and accessory structures (glands, nails, and hair) make up the integumentary system. The three layers of the skin are the epidermis, the dermis, and the subcutaneous tissue (hypodermis).

- *Epidermis* - Outer layer of skin.

- *Dermis* - Layer of skin below the epidermis and on top of the subcutaneous tissue.

- *Subcutaneous tissue* - Layer of skin below the dermis and on top of the muscle.

Younger Skin   # Older Skin

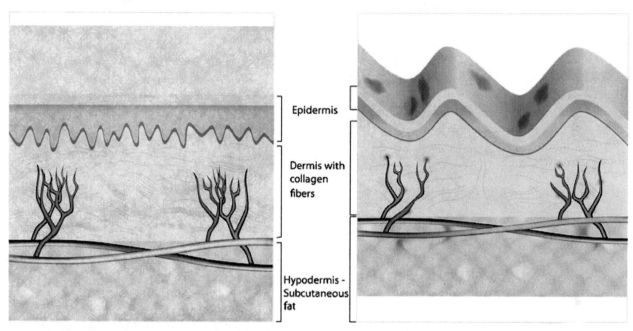

Epidermis

Dermis with collagen fibers

Hypodermis - Subcutaneous fat

Anatomy

- *Epidermis* - The epidermis is the outermost layer, and it contains four sections called stratum. The stratum basale is the deepest section.

- *Dermis* - The second skin layer is the dermis, which contains two sections: papillare and reticular. Also in the dermis are nerves, blood vessels, nails, glands, hair, and connective tissue.

- *Hypodermis* - The subcutaneous tissue contains connective tissue and fat tissue. The hypodermis connects the skin to underlying muscle.

- *Nails* - These are the keratin plates that cover each finger and toe. The lunula is the white growth area at the base of the nail plate, the eponychium is the cuticle, a narrow band at the sides and base of the nail, and the paronychium is the soft tissue around the nail border.

- *Sebaceous (Oil) Glands* - These glands are in the dermis, and they secrete oil (sebum) that lubricates the skin and hair.

- *Sudoriferous (Sweat) Glands* - These glands are in the dermis, and they secrete salty water to cool the body.

Abdominal Cavity and Organs

The abdominal cavity is separated from the thoracic cavity by the diaphragm. It is divided into four quadrants: left upper quadrant (LUQ), left lower quadrant (LLQ), right upper quadrant (RUQ), and right lower quadrant (RLQ). The abdominal organs are:

- *Esophagus* - Tube that runs from mouth to stomach and lies behind the trachea.

- *Stomach* - Digestive organ in the LUQ and receives and breaks down food.

- *Pancreas* - An organ of the RUQ that aids in digestion, produces insulin, and regulates blood sugar.

- *Liver* - A solid organ in the RUQ that helps filter toxins, break down fat, and produce cholesterol.

- *Gallbladder* - A small hollow RUQ organ that lies beneath the liver, stores bile, and releases bile during digestion.

- *Appendix* - A RLQ small organ that is often obstructed, leading to inflammation, infection, and/or rupture.

- *Spleen* - A small solid LUQ organ that filters blood.

- *Kidneys* - Two solid organs that are positioned in the mid-abdomen to control fluid, filter waste, and regulate pH balance.

- *Small intestine* - A hollow tubular organ in both lower quadrants that digests fat and releases enzymes.

- *Large intestine* - A hollow organ of the lower abdomen that pulls out liquid and forms solid stool.

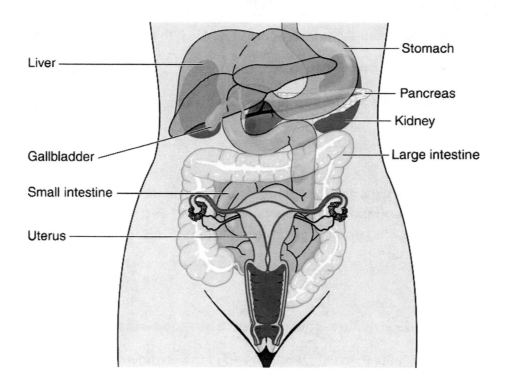

Liver

Stomach

Pancreas

Kidney

Gallbladder

Large intestine

Small intestine

Uterus

Urinary System

The urinary system controls fluid balance and filters waste from the blood via the kidneys. The ureters are two tubes that connect each kidney to the bladder. Urine moves from the kidneys, through the ureters, and then down the urethra to exit the body. This system works with the reproductive system to remove metabolic waste materials from the body, such as uric acid, urea, nitrogenous waste, and creatinine. The urinary system also maintains electrolyte balance and assists the liver in body detoxification.

Anatomy

- *Kidneys* - Two organs that control pH balance (acid/base), secrete berenin, vitamin D, and erythropoietin, and stimulate red blood cell production.

- *Cortex* - Outer layer of the kidney.

- *Medullar* - Inner portion of the kidney.

- *Hilum* - Middle section of the kidney.

- *Papilla* - Inner part of the pyramids.

- *Nephrons* - Operational units of the kidneys.

- *Ureters* - Narrow tubules that transport urine from the kidneys to the bladder.

- *Urinary Bladder* - Sac-like reservoir for the urine.

- *Urethra* - Tube that transport urine from the bladder to outside the body.

Male Reproductive System

The male reproductive organs and structures include the penis, testicles, the scrotum, epididymis, spermatic cords, seminal vesicles and ducts, the vas deferens, the bulbourethral gland, the prostate gland, and the penis. This system produces the sperm cell for reproduction.

Anatomy

- *Testes (Gonads)* - Structures that produce sperm and testosterone.

- *Vas Deferens* - Tubular structure at the end of the epididymis.

- *Prostate Gland* - Structure that produces seminal fluid and activates sperm.

- *Bulbourethral Gland* - Gland that secretes a tiny amount of seminal fluid.

- *Seminal Ducts* - Structures that transport sperm from the testes to the exterior.

- *Seminal Vesicles* - Structures that produce most seminal fluid.

- *Penis* - External genital structure that encloses the urethra and passes urine and semen.

- *Scrotum* - Sac that encloses the testes.

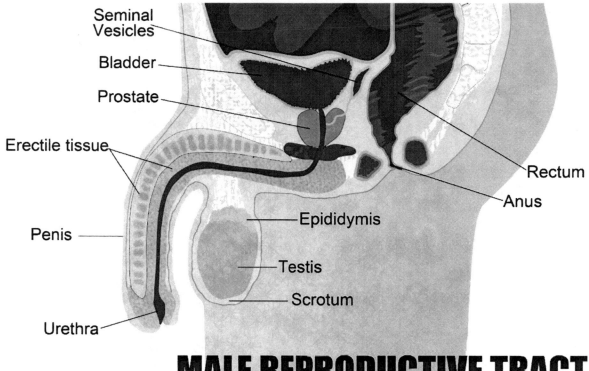

MALE REPRODUCTIVE TRACT

Female Reproductive System

The female organs are the ovaries, fallopian tubes, and the vagina. The female reproductive system protects the fertilized ovum (egg) for the nine-month gestation period. The external structures enhance sexual stimulation and protect the body from foreign materials. The internal structures produce and release the ovum.

Anatomy

- *Ovaries* - Small structures that produce ova (egg) and hormones.

- *Fallopian Tubes* - Ducts that transport ova from the ovary to the uterus.

- *Uterus* - Muscular organ with three layers: endometrium (inner mucosa), myometrium (middle layer), and perimetrium (outer layer).

- *Vulva* - External genitalia.

- *Vagina* - Cavity that spans from the uterus to outside the body.

- *Breasts* - Mammary glands and tissue that contain lactiferous ducts.

Patient safety is of utmost importance when working as an EMT-B. The service provider must use extreme caution when lifting, moving, and transferring patients. There is both a risk for injury to the provider and the patient when correct technique is not observed and followed.

Safe Lifting Techniques

- When using a power lift, keep the person or object close to his or her body and use your legs (not your back) for lifting.

- Use a power grip, where the palms are up and all fingers are firmly grasped around the object.

- Be sure to get enough help for the job.

- Prepare the lift before the process to reduce distance and avoid problems.

Emergency Moves

Emergency moves are used when the scene appears to be dangerous. The patient should be moved before giving any type of care. Emergency moves include:

- *The shirt drag* - Pulling on the patient's clothing at the shoulder or neck area.

- *The blanket drag* - Dragging or pulling the patient on a blanket.

- *The armpit-forearm drag* - Putting hands under the patient's armpits from the back, and grasping the forearms while dragging the patient.

Urgent Moves

Urgent moves are used when a patient has serious or life-threatening injuries or illnesses and need to be moved rapidly for evaluation and transport. The patient is rotated onto a blackboard and removed quickly from the vehicle. The EMS provider must use a manual cervical spine with these moves for precautionary measures. One urgent move is the rapid extrication, which is used for patients in a motor vehicle.

<u>Rapid Extrication Move</u>:

- One EMT positions behind the patient, brings the cervical spine into a neutral in-line position, and offers manual immobilization.

- A second EMT puts the patient's cervical immobilization device on as a third one places the backboard near the door.

- The second EMT supports the thorax as the third frees the patient's legs from inside the car.

- The third EMT rotates the patient until the patient's back is in the open doorway and his or her feet are on the passenger seat.

- A fourth EMT or bystander can support the patient's head as the first EMT removes the person from the vehicle.

- The second and third EMTs slide the patient into the correct position on the board.

<u>Log Roll Move:</u>

- Three trained personnel are needed for the log roll move.

- Place the patient on a backboard while observing manual cervical spine precautions.

- Keep the back straight, lean from the hips, and use shoulder muscles to help with the roll.

Non-Urgent Moves

These are necessary for patients who are not in danger and have no life-threatening illnesses or injures. Types of non-urgent moves include the direct carry method, the direct ground lift, the draw sheet method, and the extremity lift.

Non-emergency Moves

<u>Direct Ground Lift</u>

- Only use when there is no suspected spine injury.

- Two or three rescuers must line up on one side of the patient.

- One EMS provider places the patient's arms on his or her chest.

- The rescuer at the head places one arm under the patient's neck and shoulder, and then places the other under the patient's lower back.

- The second rescuer places one arm under the patient's knees and one arm above the buttocks.

- The third rescuer places both arms under the waist and the other two slide arms either up to the mid-back or down to the buttocks.

- After the signal, all three rescuers lift the patient to their knees and roll the patient toward his or her chest.

- On signal, the rescuers rise and position the patient on the stretcher.

Emergency Lift

- Used when there are no suspected injuries.

- The first rescuer knees at the patient's head with the second rescuer at the patient's knees.

- The first rescuer places one hand under the patient's shoulders, and the second one grasp the patient's wrists.

- The first rescuer slips his hands under the patient's arms and grasps the wrists.

- The second rescuer slips his hands under the patient's knees.

- Both rescuers move to a crouching position.

- The rescuers stand up together and place the patient on the stretcher.

Draw Sheet Method

- Loosen the sheet from the bottom of the bed.

- Position the cot next to the bed.

- Reach across the cot and grasp on the sheet firmly at the patient's head, chest, hips, and knees.

- Slide the patient from the cot to the bed.

Carrying Precautions

- Know the limitations of the crew's abilities.

- Work and communication with the patient and other EMS providers.

- Keep the patient's weight close to your body.

- Flex at the hips rather than the waist and bend at the knees.

- Do not hyperextend the back.

Equipment for Patient Movement

- Wheeled stretcher - The stretcher is the most commonly used piece of equipment for EMS. It is used for transport, as it is the safest way to move patients. Most units accommodate patients who are 300 pounds or less, and some have an automated lift system to reduce any risk of injury.

- Portable stretcher - A lightweight and compact stretcher, which allows more accessibility than wheeled stretchers.

- Scoop stretcher - This unit divides into two long pieces, either left and right or top and bottom. This stretcher allows for easy positioning with very little patient movement, and is good to reduce patient discomfort during transfer.

- Stair chair - This unit is great for small elevators, staircases, and household stairs. It does not allow, however, for the use of a manual cervical protection, artificial ventilation, or CPR.

- Backboard - This device is used mainly for cervical spine immobilization, and allows for CPR. It is lightweight and requires a four-person lift.

- Neonatal isolette - This unit is designed to keep neonatal patients warm while in transport, and it requires special training for operation.

Readying the Patient for Air Medical Transport

- Notify the air crew of any special circumstances, such as cardiac arrest, obese patient, traction splint use, combativeness, and/or unstable airway.

- Should there be hazardous material exposure, the patient must be decontaminated prior to entry into the aircraft.

- Secure any blankets, lose equipment, or tubing before approaching the aircraft.

- Do not approach the aircraft until the air crew authorizes this.

- Never approach a rotor wing aircraft from the rear.

Special Considerations

- *Bariatric (obese) patients* - These patients pose many risks and challenges for EMS providers during the lifting and moving process. Request additional assistance, when necessary, and decide which equipment would be best before attempting any type of movement. Many ambulances have special equipment and lifting systems to accommodate a large weight capacity.

- *Pregnant patients* - Women who are in the later stage of pregnancy should not be positioned supine due to the risk of supine hypotensive syndrome. Rather, these patients should be placed on the left side. If the female has a risk for potential cervical spine injury, the EMS provider must use a backboard to the left at a 20 degree angle.

- *Skeletal abnormalities* - Patients with odd or unusual curvature of the spine (lordosis and kyphosis) often cannot tolerate the supine lying position without padding.

Guidelines for Mechanical Restraint

- Follow laws and protocols regarding mechanical restraints.

- Restrain a patient against his or her will as a last resort.

- Request law enforcement assistance when needed.

- Contact the medical direction when possible.

- Use the minimum amount of force possible for protection of the patient, you, and others.

- Use padded, soft restraints, and avoid flex cuffs or handcuffs.

- Monitor the patient's vital signs, level of consciousness, airway, and distal circulation (below the restraints).

- Document the reason for the use of mechanical restraints, as well as the duration, method, and assessment process.

- Never restrain a patient in the prone position or leave the patient unsupervised.

Airway Management, Ventilation and Oxygen Therapy
Learning Objectives

- Understand airway assessment, suctioning, and obstructed maneuvers.

- Understand nasopharyngeal and oropharyngeal indications and procedures.

- List measures of oxygen delivery, ventilation, and pulse oximetry.

The respiratory system is made up of numerous structures in which air must pass through, including the mouth, nose, lungs, pharynx, trachea, and bronchi. These passageways are considered the airway. An obstructed airway can be dangerous if left untreated.

Breathing Physiology

Ventilation

Ventilation refers to moving air in and out of the lungs, and it is necessary for effective respiration. The active part of ventilation is inhalation. When a person inhales, the diaphragm and intercostal muscles contract along with decreased intra-thoracic pressure so a vacuum is created. With thorax enlargement, air flows through the upper airway and down to the lower airway to the alveoli.

Exhalation is a passive part of ventilation and requires no energy. With exhalation, the intercostal muscles and diaphragm relaxes, the thorax decreases and air leaves the lungs. As exhalation occurs, intra-thoracic pressure will exceed atmospheric pressure.

Regulation of Ventilation

A requirement for oxygen occurs during activity, injury, and illness, with the primary methods controlling oxygen delivery being:

- Increased or decreased breathing rate

- Increased or decreased tidal volume of breaths

Hypoxia

With hypoxia, there is inadequate delivery of oxygen into the cells. The early indications of hypoxia include tachycardia, irritability, restlessness, anxiety, and dyspnea. In the late stages of hypoxia, there is an altered level of consciousness, profound dyspnea, bradycardia, and cyanosis.

Carbon Dioxide Drive

The carbon dioxide (CO_2) drive is the body's primary system for regulating breathing. Levels of CO_2 are regulated in the blood and cerebrospinal fluid.

Hypoxic Drive

The hypoxic drive is the backup system to the CO_2 drive, and this monitors oxygen levels in the plasma. This drive is used by patients with chronic obstructive pulmonary disease (COPD) who have high levels of CO_2. Also, prolonged exposure to oxygen in high concentrations may depress spontaneous ventilations, so withholding oxygen from injured or acutely ill patients is recommended.

Respiration

The exchange of oxygen and carbon dioxide is respiration. The heart and brain become irritable at the time of injury, and brain damage can occur within four minutes. After six minutes, permanent brain damage results.

Adequate Breathing

Breathing is either adequate or inadequate. With adequate (normal) breathing, a person breathes normally, and the depth and rate of respiration is appropriate to meet the body's oxygen demands. The amount of air used to inhale and exhale in a single breath varies from person to person. Air breathed in and out is called tidal volume, and the average adult normal tidal volume is 500 ml.

Normal Respiratory Rate

- *Adults*: 12 to 20 breaths per minute

- *Children*: 15 to 30 breaths per minute

- *Infants*: 25 to 50 breaths per minute

Inadequate Breathing

Inadequate breathing can be irregular, stressed, or labored. When a person has inadequate breathing there is no breath sounds, exertional effort, and the chest may expand unequally. The signs of difficult breathing include:

- Shortness of breath

- Irregular rhythm

- Pale, cyanotic, or clammy skin

- Gasping breaths

- Nonexistent breath sounds

- Increased or decreased respirations

- Unequal, shallow chest expansion

- Retractions between ribs and above clavicles

- Alteration of consciousness

Airway Obstruction

With airway obstruction, there is blockage of an airway structure that leads to the alveoli. This leads to lack of effective ventilation. The causes of an airway obstruction include:

- Tongue (main cause of airway obstruction)

- Swelling of the throat

- Foreign bodies (toys, food, etc.)

- Fluid (blood, saliva, vomit, and mucus)

Opening the Airway

Manual Positioning

The first step to open an airway is manual positioning. The patient must be positioned on his or her back facing up. If an unconscious patient loses control of the jaw, the tongue may fall back into the throat, which causes the epiglottis to block the glottis opening and close the airway. If there is no suspected trauma, the EMT-B can use the head-tilt chin-lift technique, which keeps the airway open. This pulls the tongue out of the oropharynx and moves the epiglottis away from the glottis. Be sure to use two fingers to tilt the head backwards and lift the chin gently.

Airway Adjuncts

An airway adjunct is a small device used to keep the airway open. The two types are oropharyngeal airways and nasopharyngeal airways.

- *Oropharyngeal airway* - This is a curved plastic device that is easily inserted into the patient's mouth. It will lift the tongue from the oropharynx of unresponsive patients who have no gag reflex. Do not use this type of device if the patient has a gag reflex because it could cause vomiting or gagging.

- *Nasopharyngeal airway* - This type of device is made of flexible plastic that is inserted into the patient's nostril to give him or her an airway. A nasopharyngeal airway is a good choice for a responsive patient who needs assistance breathing, as it does not stimulate the gag reflex.

Suctioning Techniques

Once an airway is established, it may become blocked with saliva, blood, vomit, mucus, broken teeth, or food. Should this occur, the EMT-B must clear the airway so the material does not go into the lungs. The best technique to clear the airway is to roll the patient on his or her side to allow fluids to drain from the mouth.

Suction units are used to treat patients with obstructed airways. The three types are: mounted, portable, and hand-operated. These units suction materials from the patient's airway used in conjunction with a suction catheter, which is attached to the end of the tubing. Suction catheters can be either rigid or soft.

- *Rigid* - These catheters are also called tonsil tip, Yankauer catheter, or tonsil sucker. They are made from hard plastic, and can be used on unresponsive patients of any age.

- *Soft* - Also called French catheters, these are made of flexible, long plastic to clear nasal passages. It is important for the EMT-B to never insert this device farther back than the base of the tongue.

Oxygenation

Oxygenation is a delivery of oxygen to the blood, and ventilation is required for this process. Oxygenation does not necessarily produce respiration, just as ventilation does not ensure oxygenation. If a patient suffers from carbon monoxide exposure or smoke inhalation, ventilation occurs, but not oxygenation.

Artificial Ventilation

The various techniques for artificial ventilation include:

- Mouth-to-mouth

- Mouth-to-mask

- Bag-valve mask (BVM)

- Flow-restricted, oxygen-powered ventilation

Mouth-to-Mouth

Basic mouth-to-mouth artificial ventilation is a technique where the EMS provider places his or her mouth over the patient's mouth to deliver oxygen. To perform this you:

- Open the patient's mouth.

- Pinch the nose shut.

- Place your mouth over the patient's mouth.

- Exhale just enough to make the chest rise.

- Continue breaths at a rate of 1 breath every 5 seconds (1:5) for adults,1 breath every 3-5 seconds for children, and 1 breath every 3 seconds for infants.

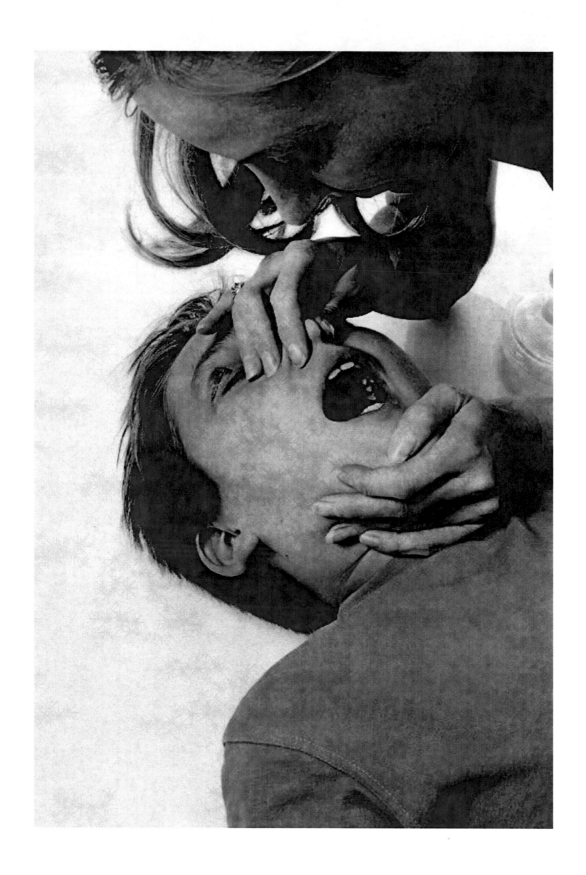

Mouth-to-Mask

Mouth-to mask ventilation employs the same basic principles as mouth-to-mouth ventilation. However, a portable pocket mask is used. These devices can be used on adults, children, and infants. The steps for using a mouth-to-mask device are:

- Clear the patient's airway.

- Insert an oropharyngeal or nasopharyngeal airway adjunct.

- Place mask over the patient's mouth.

- Connect oxygen to the mask if necessary.

- Seal the mask and place your mouth on the mask's valve.

- Exhale into the valve to make chest rise.

- Continue at the same rate as listed in mouth-to-mouth ventilation.

Bag-Valve Mask (BVM)

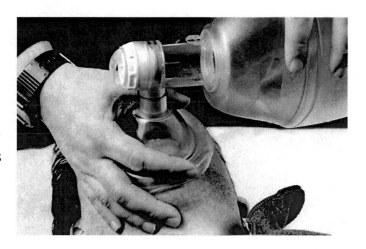

Bag-valve mask is a ventilation device that consists of using a self-inflating bag along with an oxygen reservoir, a one-way valve, and a mask. The steps for using this include:

- Clear the airway

- Insert either an oropharyngeal or nasopharyngeal airway adjunct.

- Connect oxygen to the mask.

- Place device over the patient's nose and mouth.

- Squeeze the bag to ventilate the patient.

Flow-Restricted, Oxygen-Powered Device

The flow-restricted, oxygen-powered ventilation device works similarly to the BVM. After the airway is cleared, a flow-restricted device is attached to the mask, and there is no bag. This device cannot be used on young children and infants, due to the risk of lung damage. Steps for use include:

- Keep fourth and fifth digits of your hand under the patient's jaw to lift the chin.

- Depress the button to trigger the device to administer oxygen.

- As the patient's chest rises, stop the device so the patient can exhale.

- Repeat this once every five seconds.

Oxygen

Patients often require oxygen during times of stress. The EMS provider must immediately give oxygen to any patient who experiences inadequate breathing. Oxygen is stored in the transfer vehicle in high-pressure tanks with gauges. One tank contains 2,000 pounds of pressure per square inch, and will explode if not handled properly.

Oxygen is released via valve from the tank, and a regulator is attaches to the valve. This device controls the oxygen flow from the tank to the patient. Oxygen can be delivered by nasal cannula or nonrebreather mask.

- *Nasal cannula* - Delivers low concentration of oxygen to the patient. The small piece of tubing attaches to the patient's nose, and oxygen flows directly into the nostrils.

- *Nonrebreather mask* - Delivers a high oxygen concentration, and comes in many sizes that can be attached to a bag that stores oxygen. The mask is placed over the patient's mouth and nose, and the patient must breath in the oxygen from the bag.

Patient Assessment

Learning Objectives

- Discuss methods of assessing altered mental status.

- Describe methods used for assessing if a patient is breathing.

- Describe the methods used to obtain a pulse.

- Discuss the need for assessing the patient for external bleeding.

- Describe normal and abnormal findings when assessing skin conditions.

- Describe the components of respiration.

- Identify techniques for assessing mental status.

- Describe techniques for assessing if the patient is breathing.

- Identify techniques for assessing if the patient has a pulse.

- Describe techniques for assessing the patient for external bleeding.

- Recognize techniques for assessing the patient's skin color, temperature, condition, and capillary refill.

Caring for the patient is priority, but the EMS provider must take care to assess the scene before conducting a patient assessment. The scene size-up involves scanning for safety issues that could affect the way the EMT-B responds to and cares for victims, bystanders, and other caregivers.

Scene Evaluation, Initial Assessment, and Reducing Patient Anxiety

The five components of patient assessment include scene size up, primary assessment, patient history, secondary assessment, and reassessment. The priority of each component is based on the patient's chief complaint (CC) and current condition. Trauma patients demand more primary and secondary assessment than other conscious persons. Regardless of the patient's current status, the patient assessment has to be organized and methodical.

General Information

- Biological Sex

- Race

- Estimated weight

- Age

- Chief complaint - Why EMS was called

Baseline Vital Signs

Respirations and Breathing

A person's respiratory rate is the number of breaths taken per minute. The normal respiratory rate is 12 to 20 breaths per minute. Conditions that can elevate the respiratory rate include acute respiratory distress, asthma, COPD, pneumonia, heart failure, bronchitis, and tuberculosis. Use of narcotic use, drug overdose, or a diabetic coma can lower the respiratory rate. To assess respirations:

- Look at the chest and count the respirations.

- Determine rate by counting the number of breaths in 30 seconds and multiplying by two.

- Determine the quality of breathing: normal, shallow, or labored?

    o *Normal* - Average chest wall movement and no use of accessory muscles.

    o *Shallow* - Slight chest wall movement and effort.

    o *Labored* - Increased effort to breath, use of accessory muscles, gasping and nosy, stridor, and nasal flaring.

Pulse and Heart Function

The heart beats a certain number of times each minute. This is considered the heart or pulse rate. The normal adult pulse rate at rest is from 60 to 100 beats per minute. A rapid heart rate occurs from infection, dehydration, shock, anemia, stress, anxiety, thyroid conditions, and heart conditions. A slow pulse rate can occur from certain medications (beta blockers and digoxin), a vasovagal response, and various cardiac conditions.

- Rate is the number of beats felt at the radial area multiplied by two.

- Quality can be strong, weak, irregular, regular, or absent.

- If you cannot assess radial or brachial pulse (child), use the carotid area.

- Avoid excessive pressure when assessing carotid pulse in children and the elderly.

Body Temperature

Normal body temperature is 98.6 F but the range is between 97.8 to 99.1F degrees. Body temperature can be measured with a thermometer by various routes, such as oral, axillary, forehead, or rectal. Normal body temperature is harder to control as a person gets older due to a decreased amount of subcutaneous fat below the skin. Also, aging decreases a person's ability to sweat, making them at risk for hyperthermia or heat stroke.

Elevated temperature (fever) is often a symptom of infection or inflammation, but some elderly people do not exhibit a high body temperature with illness. Conditions that often raise body temperature include infection, stress, dehydration, exercise, the environment, and thyroid disorders. When someone gets cold from weather, exposure to the elements, or experiences shock or a thyroid disorder, a drop in body temperature occurs. Any temperature of 95 F degrees or lower is defined as hypothermia.

Blood Pressure

Blood pressure has two numbers, the top is the systolic pressure, and the bottom number is a diastolic pressure. The systolic pressure is the first distinct sound of the blood flowing through the artery with the use of a blood pressure cuff. This measurement is the pressure exerted against the walls during the heart's contraction. Diastolic pressure is the sound when pressure is exerted against the walls of the arteries while the left ventricle is at rest.

Written as two numbers, a healthy blood pressure is a systolic value of 100 to 139 and a diastolic value of 60 to 79. High blood pressure is called hypertension. Factors that can elevate blood pressure include smoking, stress, exercise, eating, caffeine, certain medications, salt intake, and a full bladder. Prolonged hypertension can result in atherosclerosis, stroke, and heart failure.

Hypotension (low BP) can be caused by hypothermia, shock, and syncope. Also, older people often experience orthostatic hypotension, which occurs when standing up too quickly. Other factors that cause hypotension include arrhythmias like atrial fibrillation and bradycardia, diuretics, and digitalis.

The EMT-B can assess blood pressure by auscultation (listen for sounds), or by palpation (feeling for the pressure when the cuff is being deflated). Blood pressure is measured in all patients who are three years and older.

Skin Color Assessment

- *Pink* - Normal

- *Cyanotic* - Bluish-gray indicates inadequate oxygenation or hypoperfusion.

- *Flushed* - Reddened indicates exposure to carbon monoxide, heat, or poisoning.

- *Jaundice* - Yellow indicates liver problems, such as cancer or cirrhosis.

The EMS provider needs to consider the mechanism of injury when taking a focused history for trauma and medical patients. The EMT-B should examine the patient for injuries that may have been overlooked and wounds that are consistent with a particular mechanism of injury. These include:

- Death of a patient in the same vehicle.

- Ejection or partial ejection from a vehicle.

- Extrication time greater than 20 minutes

- Vehicle rollover with 90 degree rotation or more.

- Unrestrained patient.

- Collision resulting in 12 inches of intrusion into the passenger compartment.

Hidden Injuries

- *Seat belts* - If buckled, did they produce injuries? A seat belt does not guarantee the patient did not receive injury.

- *Air bags* - The air bags can lead to injury, and may not be effective without seat belt use. The patient can hit the steering wheel after deflation, and if left deployed, the air bag can cause deformities.

Trauma - Mechanism of Injury (Adult)

- Ejection from vehicle

- Death of passenger

- Fall greater than 20 feet

- Rollover vehicle

- Motorcycle accident

- Vehicle versus pedestrian

- High-speed crash

- Penetrations of the head, neck, chest, or abdomen

- Unresponsiveness

- Hidden injuries

Trauma - Mechanism of Injury (Child or Infant)

- Falls greater than ten feet

- Medium-speed vehicle crash

- Bicycle crash

History Assessment Techniques

OPQRST

O - Onset: When or how did the symptoms begin?

P - Provocation: What caused the symptoms or makes them worse?

Q - Quality: Describe the pain, sensations, and/or symptoms.

R - Radiation: Does sensation move to other body regions?

S - Severity: How severe is this discomfort or pain?

T - Time: How long have the symptoms persisted?

SAMPLE

S – Signs and symptoms: What are the signs and symptoms?

A – Allergies: Are you allergic to any medications, foods, chemicals, or substances?

M – Medications: Are you currently taking any prescribed or OTC medicines?

P – Past medical problems: Have you had any past or recent surgeries? Are you under the care of a physician?

L – Last oral intake: What have you had to drink or eat during the last 24 hours?

E – Events leading up to the event: What happened and what were you doing before this incident?

Assessment of Trauma Patients

DCAP-BTLS

D – Deformity

C – Contusions

A – Abrasions

P – Punctures or penetrations

B – Burns

T – Tenderness

L – Lacerations

S - Swelling

High-Risk Trauma

Adult Patients

Patients are considered high-risk if they possess certain injuries or have existing medical conditions. For adults, these include:

- A bleeding disorder
- On anticoagulant therapy
- Immunocompromised
- Respiratory or cardiovascular disease
- Older than 55 years of age

Pediatric Patients

- Fall greater than 10 feet
- Bicycle collision

Vehicle Collision

- Perform rapid trauma assessment on the patient to assess life-threatening injuries. If the patient is responsive, the symptoms should be assessed before and during the trauma evaluation.

- Consider spine stabilization.

- Consider transport awaiting arrival of ALS.

- Assess mental status

- Assess for deformities, burns, tenderness, contusions, abrasions, punctures, penetrations, lacerations, swelling, and other obvious wounds.

Scene Evaluation

When EMS providers arrive on an accident or injury site, the first thing done is to survey the scene, which is called scene size-up. Not only is scene safety important for the victim(s), but for bystanders, witnesses, and emergency personnel, as well. EMT-Bs should assess the entire scene - every visible and audible clue, as well as odors.

Body Substance Isolation (BSI)

The EMT-B must take necessary body substance isolation (BSI) precautions. BSI includes wearing appropriate protective gear, such as gloves, gowns, masks, and goggles. Always keep a spare pair of gloves in case contamination occurs. These precautions protect the EMS providers, victims, and bystanders. Personal protective equipment (PPE) is needed when there are potentially dangerous situations, such as rescue missions, hazardous materials emergencies, and violent scenes.

Hand Hygiene

To properly control and prevent infection, EMS providers must practice adequate hand hygiene. Successful hand washing requires 15 seconds or more of vigorous scrubbing, where particular attention is given to the areas around nail beds and between fingers. In addition, healthcare workers should use alcohol-based antiseptic agents (hand sanitizers) in between patients when hands are not visibly soiled and should not have artificial fingernails or nail polish when providing care.

Standard Precautions

Also called universal precautions, standard precautions hold that all patients are infected or colonized with microorganisms, whether or not there are symptoms and written diagnoses, and that a uniform level of caution should be used when caring for any given patient. Standard precautions decrease the risk of transmission of microorganisms from blood and body fluids containing blood, since many patients with HIV, hepatitis B, and hepatitis often have no visible symptoms. This set of principles is used by all healthcare workers who have direct or indirect contact with patients.

Scene Safety

Safety is necessary for everyone's well-being -- victims, bystanders, and EMS providers. Communication is a key aspect of scene safety, as the providers need to communicate various aspects of the scene. Be sure to wear PPE specified for the emergency, such as hazardous material suits, helmets, puncture-proof pants, special gloves, and ear protection.

Usually, the police on the scene will provide bystander safety, but when EMS is first to show up, it may be necessary to move people out of the way. Many times, bystanders can assist EMT-B providers with basic tasks, such as moving someone from the ground onto a stretcher. If you do this, give the bystander specific instructions for assistance.

Mechanism of Injury (MOI)

The mechanism of injury (MOI) is any incident that led to the patient's trauma, wounds, or affliction. Sometimes, this is determined prior to EMS arrival on the scene. The MOI may be uncertain in some situations, so you should attempt to determine what happened. In some instances, the MOI is spotted immediately, such as an icy road or a step of stairs. Also, if the victim is unconscious, ask any bystanders or witnesses.

Need for Additional Help and Number of Patients

After the scene has been evaluated, the EMT-B should count the number of patients and determine if there is a requirement for additional help. Sometimes, patients are not readily found, especially when there are multiple vehicles involved. Also, look for possessions that could indicate the presence of other patients, such as cell phones, wallets, or toys.

Initial Patient Assessment

The initial assessment includes evaluating mental status, breathing, airway, and circulation, as well as identifying priority patients. You will encounter questions concerning the process on EMT-B because of the initial assessment is done on every call.

General Impression

The initial assessment includes forming a general impression of the area and surroundings, as well as the patient's problems. This is done within seconds of approaching the patient. Observe the patient's general appearance, attitude, and injury. Be sure to consider the age, sex, race, and other elements to determine the nature of illness (NOI), as this applies to the chief complaint (CC).

Patient's Mental Status

The patient's mental status should be assessed immediately when the EMS providers arrive. The four categories of mental status assessment are AVPU:

- *Alert* - Does the patient respond to basic questions or the presence of the service provider?
- *Verbal* - The patient responds to the EMT-B's voice, but is unaware of the person's presence. Sometimes, when the EMT-B raises his or her voice, a change in tone will provoke a response.
- *Painful* - Does the patient respond to painful stimuli? This is often found when the provider elicits a response.
- *Unresponsive* - Does the patient respond to verbal or painful stimuli? If the patient is unresponsive, he or she should be considered for priority transport.

Patient's Airway Status

The EMS provider must determine if the airway is blocked or open. If it is occluded, it must be cleared to restore oxygen flow to the brain. Signs of obstruction of the airway include cyanosis, inability to speak, coughing, and gagging. The airway can be cleared by performing the head-tilt chin-lift method.

Patient's Breathing

Most healthy adults have a respiratory rate of 12 to 20 per minute. If the patient is breathing less than 12 breaths per minute or more than 20 breaths per minutes, have a crew member administer oxygen vial high-flow cannula or mask. If breathing ceases, open the airway and use a nonrebreather mask.

Patient's Circulation

Check the patient's pulse to determine if it the beat is strong, thready, or absent. Locate the radial pulse at the right risk region, and if not palpable, assess a carotid pulse.

Priority Patients

Certain patients are priority, so the EMT-B must identify them upon arriving to the scene. Characteristics of priority patients include:

- Severe pain

- Difficulty breathing

- Chest pain

- Uncontrolled bleeding

- Poor general impression

- Complicated childbirth

- Signs of shock

- Cannot follow instructions

- Unresponsive

Physical Examination

The patient's condition is either medical or trauma, and this will determine the type of focused physical examination required. Treating an unresponsive patient is differently from alert or conscious patients, because you must do a thorough physical exam.

Responsive Medical Patients

Medical patients must be assessed objectively and subjectively. This involves gathering detailed information regarding the onset, severity, time, provocation, and radiation of pain. Use OPQRST during this assessment, as well as SAMPLE. Also, assess vital signs, skin, pupils, circulation, and breathing.

Responsive Trauma Patient

Gathering OPQRST and SAMPLE information and performing rapid assessment is more challenging when working with trauma patients. This is due to high-pressure emergency environment and injuries. Trauma patients often have a high-risk MOI, or even an unknown MOI. Then, do a rapid head-to-toe trauma assessment to find possible hidden or internal injuries. These occur from things like ejection from a moving vehicle, a serious fall, a vehicle rollover, or penetration to the head/chest/abdomen.

Unresponsive Patients

Unresponsive patients need a head-to-toe assessment for evaluation of hidden or life-threatening conditions. You should stabilize an unresponsive patient and assume that he or she has a spinal injury. Because these patients cannot answer questions, the responder should obtain the information from family members, bystanders, and/or victims.

Ongoing Assessment

The EMT-B does an ongoing assessment on a patient when in transport. During the ongoing assessment, the provider must assess for success or failure of various interventions, such as use of oxygen. With an unstable patient, assess the situation accordingly, and report any changes to the healthcare professionals at the hospital or trauma unit.

A stable patient usually only has a simple injury, whereas an unstable patient requires more attention. The EMS provider should do ongoing assessment once every fifteen minutes for the stable patient, and every five minutes for the unstable patients.

Components of Ongoing Assessment

1. Repeat initial assessment.

2. Determine mental status.

3. Assess airway, breathing, and pulse.

4. Assess skin color, condition, temperature, and perfusion.

5. Identify priority patients.

6. Record vital signs.

7. Repeat focuses assessment.

8. Check intervention.

Assessing Geriatric Patients

The elderly are more at risk for injuries and illnesses than the general population. In the U.S., people over 65 are the fastest growing group of individuals. The aging patient often has complicated coexisting medical problems that can hamper emergency care assessment. It is vital for the EMT-B to be able to differentiate between chronic conditions associated with aging and acute changes related to injury or real illness.

Respiratory System

- Alveolar surfaces degenerate, so gas exchange is impaired.

- The pulmonary musculature is diminished in size and strength.

- Lung elasticity is often lost with age as the ribs get less pliable.

- The pulmonary system is more at risk for infection and disease.

- Aging persons have less gas exchange and loss of muscle coordination.

Cardiovascular System

- Loss of heart muscle strength leads to diminished pumping action.

- The conduction system slows with age.

- There is loss of vascular elasticity, which leads to diminished ability to dilate and constrict vessels.

- The heart must pump against higher resistance and with slowed electrical conduction.

Musculoskeletal System

- Loss of bone density due to osteoporosis.

- Progressive joint degeneration and loss of flexibility.

- Kyphosis which complicates spinal mobilization.

- Aging persons have more falls, frequent bone fractures, and injuries take longer to heal.

Neurological System

- Loss of neurons and decreased mass of brain.

- Reflexes are slowed due to nerve cell degeneration.

- Decreased night vision and loss of hearing.

- Deterioration of nervous system leads to high incidence of falls and inability to adapt to stressors.

Gastrointestinal System

- Decreased sense of smell, appetite, and thirst.

- Liver function decreased along with altered digestion.

- Intestinal tract has less peristaltic waves and less absorption of nutrients.

- Aging persons have more malnutrition and constipation due to normal aging process.

Renal System

- Loss of nephrons results in decreased kidney size and function.

- Electrolytes are often disturbed, which affect kidney filtration.

- Reduced renal blood flow occurs due to vascular stenosis.

- All changes result in decreased waste filtration, electrolyte disturbances, and the possibility of drug toxicity.

Integumentary System

- The skin becomes thin and loses elasticity.

- Skin cells do not regenerate as quickly.

- There is a loss of sense of touch.

- Changes with aging result in skin fragility and loss of protective barrier.

- Skin tears occur more often.

Leading Causes of Death in Older People

- Cardiovascular disease

- Fractures and falls

- Cancer

- Pulmonary disease

- Diabetes

- Misuse of drugs

Geriatric Patients who are at Risk

- Live alone

- Are immobile

- Are incontinent

- Have recently been hospitalized

- Have altered mental status

Communication and Documentation

The EMS provider must examine the patient and interview through communication. The bystanders and family members must be assessed as well. When gathering information, the EMT-B must document information (documentation). The notes will be either electronic or handwritten, which is legible and accurate.

Radio Communication

When the EMT-B uses the radio dispatch, be sure to state the unit's location, that you received and understand the call, and that you are responding at present. Contact the dispatcher once you reach the patient(s) and scene. Be sure to record the arrival time, when you leave the scene with the patient, when you arrive to the trauma center or hospital, and when you arrive back to your station.

The EMS service provider uses the radio to communicate with the supervisor and medical director, also. Once you complete the initial assessment and determine the patient's needs, be sure to give the physician the following information:

- Patient's CC

- Patient's age, gender, and orientation

- Patient's past medical history

- Patient's current assessment and vital signs

- What emergency care was given

- Estimated time you will be in transport

- Estimated time you will arrive at the hospital

Minimum Data Sets

EMS providers are required to obtain two sets of information when going out on a patient call: patient information and administrative information, as on the minimum data sets. Refer to the table on the following page for more details.

Patient Information	Administrative Information
Age and gender	Location and type of incident
Chief complaint	Date and time of incident report
Cause of injury and description	Date and time of EMS notification
Pre-existing conditions	Time of unit response
Signs and Symptoms	Time of EMS arrival on scene
Mental status	Time of EMS arrival to patient
Pulse and respirations	Time of EMS leaving scene
Systolic blood pressure/skin perfusion	Time of EMS at hospital
Skin color, temperature, and condition	Time of patient transfer
Emergency procedures performed	Time EMS unit back in service
Medications administered	Use of sirens and lights
Patient response to treatment	Names of crew members

Pre-hospital Care Report

The pre-hospital report is a legal document, is considered confidential, and should be not read or shared with other people. This report gives information regarding the patient's status when the EMTs arrived on the scene and as they transferred the patient. Doctors, surgeons, nurses, and insurance companies read this documentation to determine the type of care required for that person. Qualified medical personnel and anyone involved with the patient's ongoing care will also use the pre-hospital care report.

Patient Refusal Documentation

If the patient is alert, competent, and not under the influence of alcohol or drugs, he or she has the right to refuse treatment by EMS if they are called. If the provider has a concern or question regarding a patient's competence, he or she should contact the supervisor or medical director before leaving the scene. Offer the patient various alternatives to transportation to the hospital, and if the patient continues to refuse, have the medical director or the patient's primary physician speak with him or her. Before leaving the scene, the EMT-B must have the patient sign a refusal form.

Medical Emergencies

Learning Objectives

- Recognize the emergency and conduct a scene size up.

- Assess the victim: open the airway, assess breathing, and assess circulation.

- Recognize external and internal bleeding.

- Identify shock (hypoperfusion).

- Recognize anaphylaxis.

- Learn guidelines for bleeding control, hypovolemic shock, and anaphylaxis

- Recognize heart attack, angina, stroke, hyperventilation, chronic obstructive pulmonary disease, altered mental status, fainting, seizure, diabetic emergencies, and abdominal distress.

- Identify poisoning emergencies: ingested poison, alcohol, and drug emergencies, and carbon monoxide poisoning.

- Discuss emergency care for snakebites and insect stings and bites.

- Identify cold-related emergencies, nonfreezing cold injuries, freezing cold injuries, hypothermia, and dehydration.

- Recognize heat-related emergencies: water loss, electrolyte loss, effects of humidity, and heat illness.

- Explain when a situation will require emergency childbirth.

- Define the four mechanisms of injury due to motion.

- Discuss the special considerations involved with trauma patients with burns, pediatric patients, and geriatric patients.

General Pharmacology

An EMS unit often has to go out on calls related to medications and poisons. Also, the unit may be dispatched to an area of a mass casualty incident (MCI). When the unit arrives, to the staging area, the main staging officer will order EMS providers to wear PPE and treat the area as a "cold zone." If a terrorist attack is suspected, the providers must determine multiple casualties and assess patients who show signs and symptoms of salivation, lacrimation, urination, defecation, GI upset (nausea/vomiting/diarrhea), and muscle twitching, which combined is referred to as SLUDGEM.

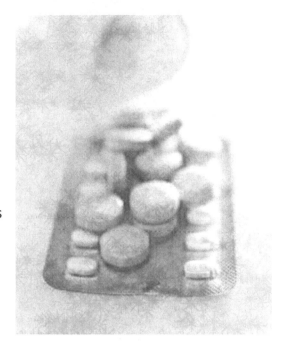

Medication names are either generic or name brand or trade brand. Generic drugs are listed in the U.S. Pharmacopeia, which is a government publication. This publication uses a simple form of the chemical name rather than the brand name. Trade (brand) drugs carry the name a manufacturer uses for marketing the drugs. An indication for a particular drug is the most common use for that medication. Contraindications for drugs are reasons the drug should not be used because it could do more harm to the patient. Also, the expiration date is a date that indicates when the medicine expired and should not be further used.

Pharmacology is the study of drugs and pharmaceuticals. The agencies that regulate drugs and drug administration are the Food and Drug Administration (FDA), which controls and regulates the drugs accepted for use in the U.S., and the Drug Enforcement Agency (DEA), which controls the administration and use specified drugs.

Drug Schedule

Schedule	Use	Example
I	Illegal or restricted to research; high abuse potential.	Marijuana and heroin
II	Medical use with limitations; high abuse potential.	Cocaine, Demerol, morphine, oxycodone, and Ritalin
III	Medical use with limitations; moderate abuse potential.	Codeine and barbiturates
IV	Medical use with limitations; low abuse potential.	Valium, Xanax, and Ativan
V	Medical use, over-the-counter, and low abuse potential.	Benadryl and Robitussin

Common Drug Routes

- *Buccal* - Placed between the cheek and gum via spray, gel, or tablet - examples: nitroglycerine and glucose

- *Inhalation* - Inhaled into the respiratory system via mists, sprays, and masks - examples: oxygen and albuterol.

- *Intradermal (ID)* - Injected into the dermal skin layer at a 15 degree angle via a 25 - 27 gauge needle - example: tuberculin skin test

- *Subcutaneous (SC)* - Injected into the subcutaneous tissue at a 45 - 90 degree angle via a 22 to 25 gauge needle - example: insulin

- *Intramuscular (IM)* - Injected into the muscle at a 90 degree angle via an 18 to 23 gauge needle - common sites for IM injections include the deltoid (upper arm), gluteus medias (the dorsogluteal area), and the vastus lateralis (thigh)

- *Intravenous (IV)* - Injected into a vein via an 18 to 22 gauge needle - example: antibiotics and fluids

- *Ophthalmic* - Placed into the eye via ointment or drops

- *Oral* - Taken by mouth and swallowed via capsule, tablet, liquid, gel, or solution

- *Otic* - Placed in the ear via drops

- *Parenteral* - Any injected medication (SC, IM, ID, or IV)

- *Sublingual* - Placed under the tongue via gel or tablets

- *Topical* - Placed on the skin via patch, ointment, cream, liquid, or spray

- *Transdermal* - Placed on the skin via patch

- *Urethral* - Placed into the urethra and bladder via a catheter

- *Vaginal* - Placed into the vagina via applicator (cream or suppository)

- *Rectal* - Placed into the anus via applicator (cream or suppository)

Six Rights of Drug Administration

- *Right patient* - Check the name and verify the patient's first and last name

- *Right drug* - Check the drug label

- Right route - Check for correct route

- Right dose - Check for the right dose

- Right time - Check for the right time to give the medication

- Right documentation - Record the medication administration in the medical record, noting date, time, drug, route, dose, site, results, tolerance, patient education, and signature of the EMT-B

Medications on the EMS Unit

Oral Glucose

- Class: Caloric

- Actions: Increase blood sugar for adequate amino acids

- Indications: Hypoglycemia

- Contraindications: Hyperglycemia

- Precautions: Hepatic and renal disease

- Side effects: Dizziness and confusion

- Dosage: One 15 gram tube

- Route: PO

Activated Charcoal

- Class: Adsorbent

- Actions: Adsorbs various toxins through chemical binding and prevents GI adsorption.

- Indications: Poisoning when emesis is contraindicated.

- Contraindications: None when there is severe poisoning.

- Precautions: Altered mental status. If ipecac was given, wait for 10 minutes before giving charcoal.

- Side effects: nausea, vomiting, and constipation.

- Dosage: 1 g/kg (50 to 75 kg) mixed with water.

- Route: PO

Oxygen

- Class: Gas

- Actions: necessary for cellular metabolism.

- Indications: Hypoxia

- Contraindications: None

- Precautions: Patients with COPD

- Side Effects: Drying of the mucous membranes

- Dosage: For cardiac arrest and critical patients, give 100%.

- Route: INH

Epinephrine (EpiPen)

- Class: Sympathetic

- Description: Epinephrine stimulates the alpha, beta-1, and beta-2 adrenergic receptors.

- Indication: Drug of choice for broncho-constrictions, hypotension from anaphylaxis, and acute allergic reaction.

- Contraindications: Hypersensitivity

- Adverse reactions: Headache, nausea, restlessness, dysrhythmia, precipitation, hypertension, and angina pectoris.

- Drug interactions: Monoamine oxidase (MAO) inhibitors and bretylium, which potentiate epinephrine.

- Supplied: Auto-injector 0.5 mg/mL (1:2000)

- Dosage: Adult 0.3mg, Pediatric 0. 15 mg

Albuterol Sulfate

- Class: Selective beta-2 adrenergic bronchodilator

- Description: Relaxes smooth muscle of the bronchial tree and the peripheral vasculature.

- Onset: Within 5 to 15 minutes

- Duration: 3 to 4 hours

- Indications: Relief of bronchospasms.

- Contraindication: History of hypersensitivity, cardiac dysrhythmias, and tachycardia caused by digitalis intoxication.

- Adverse reactions: Restlessness, tachycardia, headache, palpitations, dizziness, elevated blood pressure, hypokalemia, and dysrhythmias.

- Drug interactions: Sympathomimetics can exacerbate adverse CV effects, beta blockers antagonized albuterol, and antidepressants can potentiate vasculature effects.

- Dosage: 0.083% solution (one unit dose bottle of 3.0 mL)

MARK-I Auto Injector

The MARK-I kit has two separate auto-injectors:

- AtroPen (atropine sulfate 2 mg in 0.7 mL)

- ComboPen (pralidoxime chloride --2-PAM --600 mg in 2 mL)

Atropine

- Class: Antimuscarinic, anticholinergic, and parasympathetic blocker.

- Mechanism of action: Blocks acetylcholine (ACh) at the muscarinic receptor sites.

- Effects: The opposite of parasympathetic nervous system stimulation, as it blocks the action of the ACh.

- Heart: increases heart rate, force of contraction, and conduction.

- Lungs: Inhibits glandular section in the respiratory tract and relaxes the bronchial tree muscle for broncho-dilation.

- GI: Inhibits GI secretions and decreases motility.

- Pupils: Dilates pupils.

- GU: Decreases normal bladder tone and intensity.

Pralidoxime (2-PAM)

- Class: Antidote to cholinesterase inhibitors and organophosphate pesticides and chemicals.

- Mechanism of action: When used with atropine, it treats poisoning caused by pesticides and nerve gases.

- Side effects: Double vision, rapid breathing, dizziness, palpitations, and muscle stiffness or weakness.

Aspirin

- Class: Platelet inhibitor and anti-inflammatory agent.

- Action: Blocks platelet aggregation.

- Contraindications: People with known hypersensitivity or allergy.

- Precautions: GI bleeding and GI upset

- Side effects: Wheezing, heartburn, nausea, and vomiting.

- Dosage: 162 to 325 mg PO or chewed

- Route: PO

Nitroglycerin

- Class: Anti-anginal and vasodilator

- Description: Dilate coronary blood vessels to increase blood flow to the heart.

- Onset: 1 to 3 minutes

- Duration: 20 to 30 minutes

- Indications: ischemic chest pain, congestive heart failure, and hypertension.

- Contraindications: Hypersensitivity.

- Adverse reactions: postural syncope, transient headache, hypotension, nausea/vomiting, allergic reaction, and diaphoresis.

- Drug interactions: Other vasodilators could add to hypotensive effects.

Dosage and Administration

- Tablets - 0.15 mg, 0.3 mg, 0.4 mg, and 0.6 mg

- Aerosol - 0.4 mg metered dose

- Parenteral - 0.5 mg/mL, 0.8 mg/Ml, and 5.0 mg/mL

- Topical - 2% cream or ointment

Forms of Medications

- Gels - Insta-glucose

- Tablets and compressed powders - Nitroglycerin

- Suspensions - Activated charcoal

- Sublingual spray - Nitroglycerin

- Liquid for injection - Epinephrine

- Fine inhalation powder - Atrovent inhaler

- Liquid for nebulizer – Albuterol

Common Drug Terms

- Dose - How much needs to be given.

- Administration - Route the medication is administered.

- Actions - Desired effects of a drug.

- Side effects - List of actions that the drug could cause that are not favorable.

- Sublingual (SL) - Under the tongue

- Oral (PO) - By mouth

- Injectable (SC/IM/IV) - Given by injection

- Inhalation (INH) - Given through breathing

- Topical (TOP) - Applied to the skin.

Asthma

Asthma is a chronic respiratory condition that many EMS providers must treat from time to time. This common illness is characterized by airway inflammation that has two phases of responses. During the first phase, fluid leads from the capillaries and that leads to bronchial constriction and reduced expiratory air flow. With the second phase, the swelling cases further difficulties with expiratory flow of air, and this often occurs around 6 to 8 hours after the onset of the asthma attack.

The EMT-B must receive permission to threat the patient when responding to the scene. Common inhalers used are albuterol, isoetharine, and metaproterenol. The patient should be showing signs of respiratory distress before these inhalation therapies are given.

COPD

Chronic obstructive pulmonary disease (COPD) is a category of lung diseases that includes emphysema, asthma, and chronic bronchitis. With emphysema, there is lung damage from cigarette smoking that causes the alveolar surface area to decrease and gas exchange to diminish. Many patients with this chronic form of COPD have a prolonged expiratory phase and increased red blood cell production, which gives the skin a pinkish tone (pink puffers).

Chronic bronchitis results from excessive mucus production in the respiratory tract. The alveoli often become obstructed by mucus clogs, and the patient can become cyanotic and swollen (blue bloaters). The EMS provider will often have to administer oxygen to COPD patients who are in distress.

Airway Obstruction

Upper airway obstruction occurs from blockage of the trachea, voice box, and throat. Many causes of this include allergic reactions, burns, infections, trauma, aspiration of foreign bodies, or blockage from the tongue. Lower airway obstruction is when there is blockage of the lower trachea or lungs. This often occurs from mucus or fluid buildup or directly from inflammation.

Respiratory Distress

Respiratory distress occurs when respiratory distress causes the body to require more oxygen. The main symptom of respiratory distress is difficulty breathing, but other symptoms can be increased respiratory rate, altered rhythm of breathing, and reduced quality or depth of breathing. This can result in retention of carbon dioxide and inability to utilize oxygen.

Patients who are experiencing respiratory distress often exhibit poor breathing quality, unequal or diminished breath sounds, and unequal chest expansion. Patients often have altered tidal volume, a high pulse rate, altered mental status, changes in skin color, use of accessory muscles, and restlessness.

Respiratory Failure

When a patient is in respiratory failure, the lungs are unable to function properly, and the patient cannot take in adequate oxygen. Also, carbon dioxide is often retained when this occurs.

Assessment of Respiratory Disorders

- SAMPLE and OPQRST history.

- Physical examination.

- Assess presenting signs and symptoms.

- Look for hyperinflation of the chest.

Management of Respiratory Disorders

- Administer medications per protocol.

- Maintain the patient's airway.

- Use cervical spine collar if trauma is suspected.

- Hypoxic patients should receive high-concentrated oxygen.

- Remove anything that causes airway compromise.

- If choking, encourage coughing.

- If the patient is unable to speak and choking, perform abdominal thrusts.

- For an unconscious patient, remove blockage and administer CPR.

- Administer medications per protocol.

Conditions that Present as Dyspnea

- Common cold - This is a viral illness that can lead to mild dyspnea.

- Pneumonia - Can be viral or bacterial, and is an infection that leads to fluid accumulation in the interstitial space between the alveolus and capillary.

- Croup - More common among young children 3 years and younger, this is an inflammation of the lining of the larynx. It is characterized by a "seal bark" and dyspnea.

- Epiglottitis - A bacterial infection of the epiglottis that produces swelling and shortness of breath. This condition is considered life-threatening, and should be treated at the hospital.

Inadequate Circulation

Shock (hypoperfusion) is a profound depression of the body's vital processes. It is characterized by signs and symptoms of paleness, cyanosis, cool clammy skin, shallow and rapid breathing, rapid but weak pulse, mental dullness, restlessness, and anxiety. Also, there is a reduction in blood volume, so low or decreasing blood pressure is seen, as is subnormal body temperature.

Cardiac Compromise

- Feeling of impending doom

- Squeezing, chest pain or dull pressure that may radiate down the arm or to the jaw.

- Sudden onset of diaphoresis (sweating)

- Anxiety and irritability

- Difficulty breathing

- Irregular or abnormal pulse rate

- Abnormal blood pressure

- Epigastric pain

- Nausea and/or vomiting

Acute Coronary Syndrome (ACS)

The symptoms of ACS are from myocardial ischemia. This syndrome includes both angina pectoris and acute myocardial infarction (heart attack). Angina is transient chest pain that results from a lack of oxygen to the heart muscle. This can occur at rest or during physical activity or stress. It resolves with rest, oxygen, and nitroglycerine. Angina only last around 5 to 15 minutes, and does not cause permanent heart damage.

With acute myocardial infarction (MI), there is actual death to a region of the cardiac muscle from lack of oxygenated blood flow, usually from blocked coronary arteries. The symptoms of angina and MI are similar, but MI pain atypically does not go away after a few minutes. The EMS provider should treat the patient with chest pain as if he or she is having an MI.

Electrocardiogram

An electrocardiogram (EKG or ECG) is a noninvasive test that records the electrical activity of the heart and detects cardiac dysrhythmias. EMS provider interventions for electrocardiography include reassuring the patient that there will be no electrical shock and instructions on normal breathing.

Electrocardiography involves heart activity. The electrical activity of the heart follows a conductive pathway resulting in the cardiac cycle (heart pumping blood). There are three types of cardiac polarity: polarization, depolarization, and repolarization. Polarity is the electrical status of cardiac muscle cells in an attempt to maintain electronegativity inside the cells for distribution of ions, such as potassium, sodium, and chloride. Polarization is resting of the cardiac muscles cells, depolarization is charging and contracting of these cells, and repolarization is recovery of the cells.

The cardiac cycle involves pumping to the heart in a rhythmic cycle of contraction and reaction. Normally, the adult heart beats between 60 to 100 beats each minute, which are considered cycles. The phases of contractions are called systole and the phases of relaxation are called diastole.

Cardiac Arrhythmias

Cardiac arrhythmias are irregular heart activities, which include:

- Bradycardia - Slow heartbeat (less than 60 beats per minute).

- Tachycardia - Fast heartbeat (more than 100 beats per minute).

- Asystole - Absence of a heart rate (flat line).

- Ectopic beat - A beat that originates outside of the heart's pacemaker (SA node).

- Premature ventricular contraction (PVC) - A contraction of ventricles that occurs early.

- Ventricular fibrillation - Uncoordinated ventricular contractions (quivering of the heart).

- Ventricular flutter - A ventricular rate of 150 to 300 beats per minute (considered life-threatening).

- Premature atrial contraction (PAC) - Atrial contraction that occurs early.

- Paroxysmal atrial tachycardia (PAT) - Atrial tachycardia that occurs and subsides suddenly.

- Atrial fibrillation - Atrial rate of 350 to 500 beats per minute

- Atrial flutter - Atrial rate of 250 to 350 beats per minute that produces a "saw tooth" pattern.

Normal and Pathological Electrocardiograms

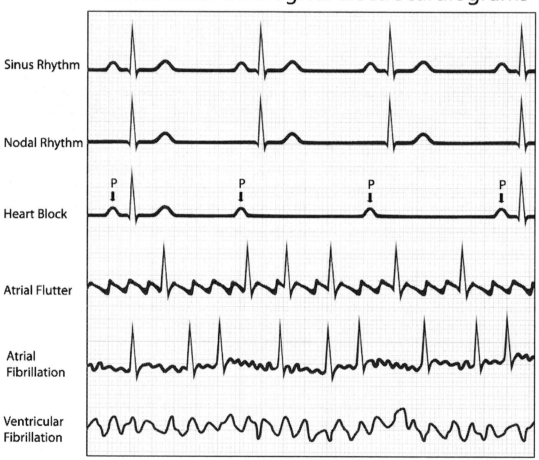

Congestive Heart Failure (CHF or HF)

With congestive heart failure, the ventricles are not able to adequately pump blood or handle the blood pumped into them. With right ventricular failure, the blood backs up into the venous system, causing jugular venous distension (JVD) and leg/foot swelling (edema). With left ventricular failure, the blood backs up into the lungs, causing pulmonary edema. Symptoms include dyspnea, chest pain, leg and foot swelling, and difficulty breathing lying down (orthopnea).

Hypertension (HTN)

Also called high blood pressure (HBP), hypertension is a reading of anything above 140 mmHg systolic pressure or above 90 mmHg diastolic pressure. A hypertensive crisis is when the blood pressure is either over 160 systolic or over 94 diastolic. Signs of this include ringing of the ears (tinnitus), headache, nausea/vomiting, nosebleed, and dizziness.

Fluid and Electrolyte Imbalances

Fluid compartments of the body include the intravascular, intracellular, and extracellular areas. The intravascular compartment is fluid inside a blood vessel, the intracellular compartment is the fluid inside the cell, and the extracellular compartment is the fluid outside the cell in the interstitial space or transcellular areas (peritoneal, pleural, cerebrospinal, and synovial). Third-spacing of fluid occurs when there is accumulation and trapped extracellular fluid in a body space, such as joint cavities, the pleural spaces, or within soft tissues. Edema is excess fluid in the interstitial spaces, from cardiac or liver failure, or localized, from burns or traumatic injury.

Electrolytes are substances that exist in the human body, dissolve in solution, and have electrically charged atoms or ions. When there is fluid loss, the body loses electrolytes. The kidneys play a major role in regulating fluid and electrolyte balance, with the quantity of fluid determined by the amount of water ingested and the amount of waste excreted.

Homeostasis is the medical term that indicates relative stability of the internal body fluid balance. Fluid volume deficit is dehydration, which occurs when the fluid intake is not sufficient for the body. Dehydration is caused by inadequate fluid intake, fluid shifts between compartments, increased fluid loss from perspiration, diarrhea, and ketoacidosis, renal failure, chronic illness, and chronic malnutrition. Fluid volume deficit is corrected by administration of IV fluids, use of antidiarrheal medications, and treatment of the electrolyte imbalance, if necessary.

Fluid volume excess occurs from overhydration, where fluid intake and retention exceeds the body's requirements. The goal of treatment is to correct electrolyte imbalances if present, eliminate the underlying cause of the overload, and restore fluid balance. Care interventions include stabilizing and monitoring for complications.

Patient Assessment and Management

Any patient with chest pain or any cardiac emergency should be transported as high priority. The EMT-B should consider medications such as nitroglycerine and aspirin per standard EMS protocol and with approval of the medical director. Also, consider us of continuous positive airway pressure (CPAP) or bi-level positive airway pressure (BIPAP) for patients in heart failure.

Administering Oxygen

When the EMS provider confirms a patient is experiencing cardiac compromise, he or she should administer oxygen after placing the patient in a comfortable position. The oxygen can be given through a nonrebreather mask at a rate of 15 liters per minute.

Nitroglycerine Use

Most protocols allow EMT-B providers to administer nitroglycerine tables or sublingual sprays for person who have chest pain and who have a doctor's prescription. Before giving this drug, determine what doses the patient took before you arrived. Most protocols require you to contact medical director if the patient does not have a prescription.

After giving the nitroglycerine, the patient should be monitored for changes in blood pressure and LOC. If the patient experiences a systolic BP of less than 100, place him or her in the Trendelenburg position and reassess.

Defibrillation

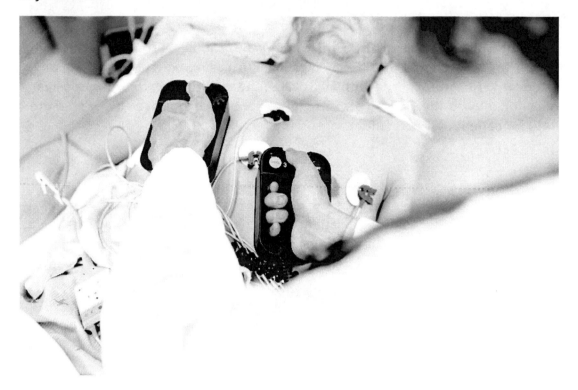

Defibrillation is used for emergency treatment for patients who are in ventricular fibrillation, a form of irregular heartbeat. Also called v. fib, this arrhythmia is characterized by rapid electrical impulses. Defibrillation involves administering and electric shock to the heart with the purpose of reestablishing a normal rhythm. CPR is often performed along with defibrillation.

The automated external defibrillator (AED) is a computer-controlled device that requires little manipulation for use. EMT-B providers can use the AED to administer life-saving treatment. The semi-automatic AED involves placement of patches and leads, so the user can analyze the rhythm. To administer a shock, only a push of a button is necessary. The fully automatic AED is quicker, and usually the preferred device.

Altered Mental Status and Diabetic Emergencies

Diabetics, seizure patients, and stroke victims often have an altered mental status. This is where the patient's verbal and/or nonverbal response shows that he or she is unaware of the current circumstances. Altered mental status occurs with diabetic patients frequently. A glucometer is used to assess capillary blood glucose levels. Normal readings are between 80 to 120 mg/dL, but less than 140 is considered normal after eating. Hypoglycemia is a reading of 60 or less, and hyperglycemia is when the level stays above 140 persistently.

Hypoglycemia

Hypoglycemia is where the body's blood glucose levels are low, and this makes the patent appear intoxicated. Symptoms can be slurred speech, staggering, or unresponsiveness. If left untreated, hypoglycemia can result in seizures, coma, and even brain death.

Insulin Shock

Insulin shock is the medical term that refers to sever hypoglycemia with signs and symptoms. This is often caused when a patient take insulin and doesn't eat, or from excessive physical activity without adjustment of insulin or food intake. Symptoms of this include diaphoresis, tachycardia, cool and clammy skin, pallor, restlessness, and altered LOC.

Hyperglycemia

Hyperglycemia is a sustained elevated blood glucose level, usually of 140 mg/dL or above. This causes the patient to have excessive thirst, dry mouth, thirst, and irritability. Hyperglycemia comes on slowly and is not dangerous unless glucose levels continue to rise.

Diabetic Ketoacidosis (DKA)

More common for patients with type 1 diabetes, diabetic ketoacidosis (DKA) is when the glucose level goes above 350 mg/dL. The body will spill glucose into the urine and excrete it rapidly, which leads to dehydration. The symptoms and signs of DKA include Kussmaul respirations (deep, long, rapid breathing), the three Ps (polydipsia, polyphagia, and polyuria), unusual breath odor, tachycardia, and coma.

Indication	Hypoglycemia (below 60)	Hyperglycemia (over 400)
Breath	No change	Fruity or sweet odor
Skin	Cold and clammy	Warm and dry
Behavior	Irritable, tremors, and/or confused	Drowsiness, fatigue, and or lethargy
Level of consciousness	May become unresponsive	Disoriented or coma
GI system	Hunger and nausea	Nausea, vomiting, and thirst
Pulse	Normal or elevated	Weak and rapid
Onset of symptoms	Rapid	Slow

Patient Assessment and Management

For patients with low blood glucose, they must be given some form of oral glucose to raise the sugar level and reverse the condition of hypoglycemia. EMT-B providers can administer this, but oral glucose cannot be given to an unresponsive patient.

Stroke

A stroke is when there is brain tissue death from interruption in blood flow. Also called a cerebrovascular accident (CVA), current treatment for stroke can drastically reduce the amount of damage this condition causes. Ischemic strokes, the most common type, occur when there is blockage of blood flow to the brain, such as with atherosclerosis. Hemorrhagic strokes are caused by bleeding within the brain itself, and that bleeding affects oxygen flow and puts pressure on the brain tissue.

Atrial Fibrillation and Stroke

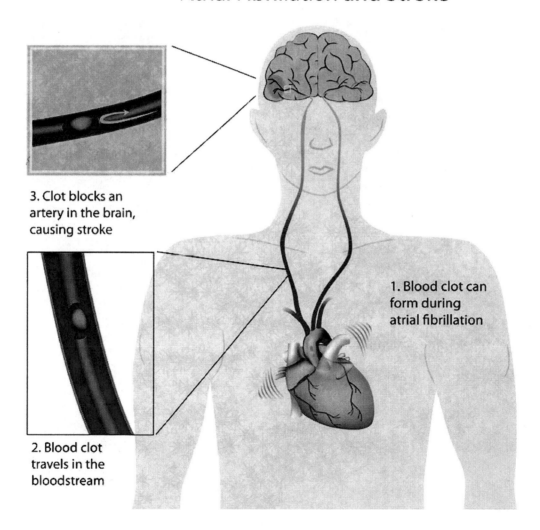

3. Clot blocks an artery in the brain, causing stroke

2. Blood clot travels in the bloodstream

1. Blood clot can form during atrial fibrillation

Signs and Symptoms of Stroke

The signs and symptoms of a stroke include:

- Facial drooping and drooling

- Severe headache

- Slurred speech,

- One-sided (unilateral) numbness, weakness, and/or paralysis

- Altered LOC

- Visual disturbances

- Trouble walking or moving

Transient Ischemic Attack (TIA)

A transient ischemic attack (TIA) often has the same presentation as a CVA. However, the symptoms and signs often resolve before 24 hours with no residual damage. Also called mini strokes, a TIA is a warning sign of an impending stroke.

Seizures

A seizure occurs when there is disorganized electrical activity of the brain. There are several types of seizures. These include:

- *Generalized seizure* - Also called a grand mal seizure, this type causes unresponsiveness and full body convulsions.

- *Absence seizure* - Also called petit mal seizure, this type does not cause convulsions, and the patient does not interact with the environment.

- *Partial seizure* - With this type, there is no change in LOC, but the patient may have twitching and sensory changes.

- *Complex partial seizure* - This type causes sensory changes, twitching, and altered LOC.

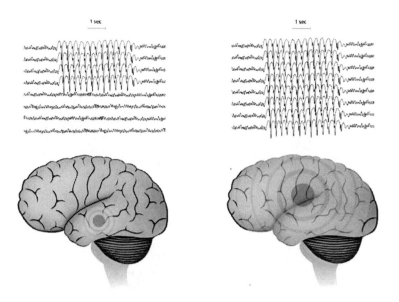

Partial seizure   Generalized seizure

Syncope

Syncope is the medical term for passing out or fainting. This is caused by a temporary loss of blood flow to the brain, as can result from hypotension, anemia, pregnancy, stress, a cardiac issue, or toxin exposure. Patients usually regain consciousness as soon as they are positioned in supine or Trendelenburg position.

Headache

A severe headache can occur from a stroke, hypertension, an aneurysm, a brain tumor, trauma, meningitis, or migraine. Symptoms vary according to headache cause, but often include head pain, elevated blood pressure, stiff neck, and neurological impairment.

Patient Assessment and Management

Any patient suspected of having a stroke or TIA should be considered high transport priority. The EMT-B should protect the patient during transport from further harm or injury.

Seizure patients should be positioned in the lateral recumbent position for airway protection. If vomiting occurs, the long board must be tilted.

When a patient comes in contact with a foreign substance (antigen), the immune system detects this and deploys antibodies to fight the antigens. This can be in the form of absorption, ingestion, injection, or inhalation.

Allergic Reaction

An allergic reaction is when there is an excessive immune reaction to an allergen or antigen. These can be local or systemic. Symptoms of an allergic reaction include rash to the skin, hives, watery eyes, itching, runny nose, and sneezing. Severe reactions progressively worsen over time.

Anaphylaxis

Also known as anaphylactic shock, anaphylaxis is a severe and life-threatening type of allergic reaction. When this occurs, the patient has impairment of the airway, respiratory system, and cardiovascular system. Symptoms include airway swelling, increased mucus production, bronchoconstriction, hypotension, capillary leakage, flushed skin, hives, restlessness, irritability, dyspnea, wheezing, stridor, tachypnea, and hypotension. The image at right is of hives that develop on the skin.

Anaphylaxis Causes

- *Medications* - Including antibiotics, non-steroidal anti-inflammatory drugs (NSAIDs), aspirin, and even vitamins
- *Environmental agents* - Such as pollen, mold, dust, or chemicals.
- *Foods* - Including peanuts, shellfish, and eggs.
- *Latex* - Found in most medical supplies.
- *Bites and stings* - From wasps, bees, spiders, ants, and other insects.

Patient Assessment and Management

The first line of treatment for anaphylaxis is epinephrine, given per local protocol. Many patients often require oxygen administration, as well. When you assess the patient with an allergic reaction, determine the exact cause and attempt to remove it from the situation.

Snake Bites and Bee Stings

When a patient sustains a snake bite, the EMT-B must assess for the risk of envenomation. Signs of a poisonous snake are depressions between each eye of the snake, as well as curved fangs, swelling at the site, and secretions on the skin after the bite. If a patient sustains a snake bite from a poisonous snake, the first measure is to apply a constricting band proximal to the fang marks.

Poisonous snakebites can cause hemoptysis, hematuria, petechia, and extensive bruising from disseminated intravascular coagulation. A bite from a pit viper can cause tissue necrosis, massive tissue swelling, hypovolemic shock, and renal failure. A bite from a coral snake will cause mild, transient pain at the bite site, cranial and peripheral nerve defects, nausea, vomiting, and total flaccid paralysis.

If a patient is allergic to bee stings, he or she will experience swelling at the sting site, wheezing, laryngeal edema, deterioration in mental status, and labored rapid breathing. Treatment for an anaphylactic reaction involves administration of 1.5 mL of 1:1000 epinephrine intramuscular. The patient also needs an intravenous line and cardiac monitoring. The EMS provider should instruct the patient to wear a medical alert bracelet, carry an EpiPen, and be cautious of areas where bees are likely to live.

Poisoning and Overdose

Poisonings and overdoses are common types of medical emergencies seen by EMS providers. This occurs when the patient ingests or is exposed to a toxic substance. Toxins cause negative effects in the body, and poisoning can result from an overdose on medication, both prescribed and obtained illegally.

- Ingested toxins - Consumed orally, such as cleaning products or mushrooms. These cause diarrhea, nausea, vomiting, abdominal pain, and cramps.

- Inhaled toxins - Breathed into the body via the respiratory tract, and can result in chest pain, coughing, stridor, and hoarseness. One common inhaled toxin is carbon monoxide.

- Injected toxins - These substances enter the body through skin punctures or direct administration by the patient. Examples are snakebites, bee stings, and medications/drugs. Symptoms include dizziness, weakness, nausea, vomiting, fever, and chills.

- Absorbed toxins - These enter the body though the skin and cause itching, redness, burning, and swelling. Examples include dyes, pesticides, and chemicals.

Patient Assessment and Management

When you find the patient, remove the source of toxin if necessary. Also, decontaminate the patient when required. Because many toxins and substances affect the airway and breathing, it is important to monitor these at all times while the patient is in transport. Activated charcoal can be given for some patients who meet certain criteria. EMS providers should contact the medical director before treating patients who have ingested poisons.

Poison Safety Measures

A poison is any substance that destroys or impairs health or life when inhaled, ingested, or otherwise absorbed by the body. The reversibility of the poison effect is determined by the capacity of the body tissue to recover from the poison. Poisonous substances can alter various body systems, including the respiratory, central nervous, circulatory, hepatic, renal, and gastrointestinal systems. Safety measures include:

- Keep the Poison Control Center phone number visible.

- Remove obvious substances/materials from patient's mouth, eyes, or body area.

- If the patient vomits, save the vomitus for examination.

- Never induce vomiting unless specified in poison control policies.

- Never induce vomiting in an unconscious patient.

Acute abdominal pain can occur from trauma, inflammation, distention, or ischemia. The types of abdominal pain are visceral and parietal. Visceral pain is dull and diffuse, difficult to localize, often associated with nausea and vomiting, and is often indicative of organ damage. Parietal pain is localized, severe, sharp, constant, and causes the patient to wince and appear uncomfortable.

Appendicitis

Appendicitis is caused by an inflamed appendix, and it can lead to a life-threatening infection and septic shock. Most patients will complain of severe right lower quadrant abdominal pain.

Peritonitis

Peritonitis is the result of an inflamed peritoneum, which is the membrane lining the abdominal organs and cavity. Most patients will present with nausea, vomiting, diarrhea, and fever.

Cholecystitis

Cholecystitis is gall bladder inflammation, which can be the result of gallstones. It often occurs in women age 30 to 50 years, and leads to upper right quadrant pain, nausea, vomiting, and referred discomfort to the shoulder.

Diverticulitis

With diverticulitis, there are inflamed and infected diverticula (small pouches of the intestines). This mostly affects older people, and leads to weakness, lower abdominal pain, fever, nausea, and vomiting.

Gastrointestinal (GI) Bleeding

GI bleeding occurs in middle-aged persons, and can be fatal for many geriatric persons. Most upper GI bleeding is due to ulcers, whereas lower GI bleeding occurs from diverticulitis. Symptoms include vomiting blood, blood in the stool, and hypovolemic shock with excessive blood loss.

Abdominal Aortic Aneurysm (AAA)

When the wall of the aorta in the abdomen weakens, an abdominal aortic aneurysm (AAA) can develop. This is often common in geriatric men, and a ruptured AAA is often fatal due to massive blood loss. The symptoms include tearing back pain, pulsating abdominal mass, and hypovolemic shock.

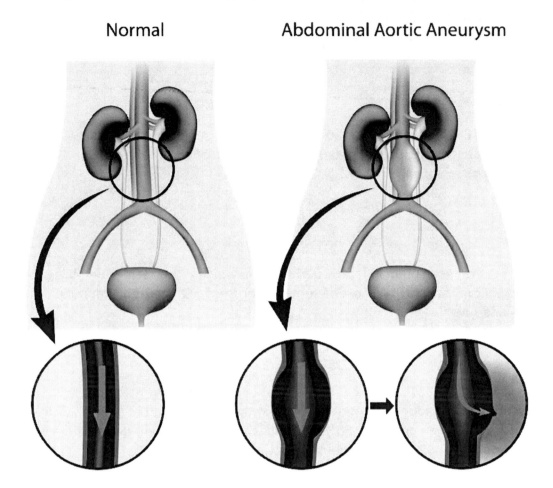

Normal   Abdominal Aortic Aneurysm

Kidney Stones

Renal calculi (kidney stones) occur when crystals form in the kidneys and cause obstruction. Men have kidney stones more frequently that women, and they lead to severe abdominal and back pain, groin discomfort, painful urination, nausea, vomiting, and fever.

Kidney Failure

Kidney failure occurs when a patient's kidneys can no longer function adequately. With this condition, waste products, toxins, and water all accumulate in the body.

Dialysis is the artificial removal of excess fluid and waste products from the body, and this is often a required treatment for kidney failure.

Patient Assessment and Management

The EMS provider should be cautious with patients who complain of abdominal pain. Patients at risk for various serious conditions include:

- Women of child-bearing age who have abdominal pain.

- Any person with bleeding, vomiting, syncope, trauma, or signs of shock.

- Patient who have severe back or flank pain.

- Geriatric and diabetic patients.

Environmental emergencies are injuries and illnesses that occur from the outdoor environment. These are related to weather, water, or harm from various animals and insects. A thermoregulatory emergency occurs when a patient endures a significant decrease or increase in basal body temperature.

Hypothermia

The body loses heat by five basic mechanisms: conduction, convection, evaporation, respiration, and radiation.

- *Conduction* - Direct transfer of heat through contact with a cold surface, such as the floor or ground.

- *Convection* - Loss of heat to passing air, such as a cold breeze.

- *Evaporation* - Loss of heat through water evaporation through the skin, such as getting out of a warm pool or shower.

- *Respiration* - Exhaled air is warmed within the body in a cold environment, but that heat is lost with exhalation.

- *Radiation* - Direct transfer of radiant heat, as with walking into a freezer.

Hypothermia is a condition where there is excessive exposure to cold climates, and the body temperature falls well below 98.6 degrees F. Generalized hypothermia affects the entire body, with the main signs being altered mental status and impaired motor function. The body attempts to raise the temperature by elevating both heart and respiratory rates.

The signs and symptoms of hypothermia include pale or cyanotic skin, shivering, stiff muscles, difficulty speaking, and altered LOC. The patient may have hypotension, bradycardia, and bradypnea (slow breathing) as well.

Frostnip and Frostbite

Frostnip develops when certain parts of the body get extremely cold, but are not yet frozen. Also called chilblains, frostnip symptoms and signs include pale, cold skin and loss of sensation in affected area. Frostbite is a dangerous local cold emergency where the tissue becomes frozen, and this often leads to permanent damage (gangrene). The signs and symptoms of frostbite include hard, frozen body tissue, possible mottling, and occasional blistering.

Hyperthermia

Hyperthermia occurs when a patient's body temperature rises and is sustained well above 98.6 degrees F. This is most common in humid, hot weather, and dehydration is a contributing factor for hyperthermia. The symptoms of this condition include dizziness, weakness, muscle cramps, rapid heartbeat, nausea, vomiting, and altered mental status.

Heat-related illnesses are preventable by limiting activities during the peak sun hours of 10 a.m. and 4 p.m., wearing loose-fitting clothes, and staying hydrated. Exertional heat occurs when running or exercising in hot climates which makes body temperature rise. First aid measures for heat stroke include placing ice on the neck, chest, axillae, and groin, removing clothes, and wetting the patient with tepid water. Older adults are at increased risk for heat-related illnesses.

Heat Exhaustion

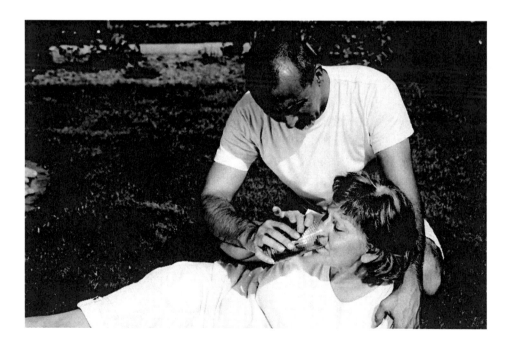

One systemic heat emergency that occurs occasionally is heat exhalation, which is caused by hypovolemia and heat exposure. The signs and symptoms of this condition include dizziness, weakness, tachycardia, headache, thirst, muscle cramps, nausea, and vomiting.

Heat Stroke

One extremely dangerous and uncommon systemic heat emergency is heat stroke. This occurs when the body loses the ability to regulate heat, and the temperature rises rapidly. If untreated, heat stroke will lead to death. The signs and symptoms of heat stroke include altered or decreased LOC, seizures, dizziness, weakness, tachycardia, headache, thirst, muscle cramps, nausea, and vomiting.

Predisposing Factors of Heat Stroke

- High humidity

- Obesity Seizures

- Dehydration

- Beta-adrenergic blockers

Near-Drowning and Drowning

Near-drowning incidents can occur when a victim strikes an object while engaging in water sports, such as skiing or swimming. This is when a patient survives an immersion event. These injuries usually involve spinal trauma, so the patient should be immobilized. A near-drowning victim will require fluid removal from the airway, and artificial ventilation is used during transport.

Drowning is actual death that results from immersion in water. Water rescue is extremely hazardous, so the EMT-B must have specialized training for this, such as lifeguards receive.

Patient Assessment and Management

For hypothermia, the EMS provider must first check the pulse to determine if the patient has severe bradycardia or is in cardiac arrest. The patient should be immediately moved from the cold environment, and all wet clothes should be removed to prevent further body temperature loss. Pre-hospital warming only involves the use of blankets, as rapid rewarming can lead to ventricular fibrillation.

For hyperthermia, the EMS provider should apply cool packs to the patient's neck, armpits, and groin. Also, all excessive clothing should be removed as the patient is in transport to the hospital. If a patient has a local cold emergency, remove jewelry, bandage or splint the affected area, keep the patient immobile, and avoid rubbing the affected area(s) Also, do not apply direct heat unless authorized by the medical director.

Management for systemic heat emergencies involve moving the patient to a cooler environment, giving him or her water and taking aggressive cooling measures. The patient should be cooled with cold packs, wet towels, or water. Also, the EMT-B should be prepared for possible vomiting and seizures.

For near-drowning, or drowning injuries, the patient is at risk for cardiac arrest, hypothermia, aspiration, and cervical spine injury. Threat the patient under consultation with the medical director.

Behavioral emergencies involve any unacceptable behavior, and they can be physiological or psychological. The physiological causes include drugs, alcohol, toxins, seizures, diabetic emergencies, head injury, and hypoxia. The psychological causes are more complex and include:

- *Anxiety* - From stress-related to an event or circumstances.

- *Depression* - Profound sadness and suicidal ideation.

- *Bipolar disorder* - Drastic mood changes and mania.

- *Paranoia* - Extreme suspicion and/or distrust of others.

- *Psychosis* - A state of delusion.

- *Phobias* - Fear of something, someone, or an entity.

Suicidal Patients

Females are more likely to attempt suicide, but males are more likely to actually go through with it. These attempts often involve drugs, firearms, and other means of harming the self. Risk factors include recent divorce, loss of spouse, mental illness, previous suicide attempt, drug abuse, serious illness, or loss of job.

Bereavement, Grief, Death, and Loss

Bereavement is the period of mourning. The amount of time varies from person to person, but typically lasts six to twelve months, and in some cases, longer. Grief is a normal response to loss, and mourning is the public expression of grief. The three types of grief are acute, chronic, and anticipatory. With chronic grief, the person is at risk for depression, which is characterized by feelings of sadness and changes in mood.

Loss is the absence of something wanted, available, and loved. With actual loss, others can identify a situation or event, whereas with perceived loss, the patient experiences something others cannot comprehend or verify. Anticipatory loss is when the patient expects and experiences the loss before it occurs.

The EMS provider's role concerning grief and loss involves assisting the patient with various feelings and adjustments. Adequate communication with the patient and family is necessary, as is provision of counseling and referrals to mental health professionals. The EMT-B must consider the survivor's religion, culture, family dynamics, coping skills, and support systems.

Stages of the Grief/Loss Response

- *Stage 1: Shock and Disbelief* – The survivor feels numb, has emotional outbursts, denies the situation or event, and isolates self.

- *Stage 2: Experiencing the Loss* – The survivor feels angry regarding the loss/death, bargains regarding this event, and suffers from depression.

- *Stage 3: Reintegration* – The survivor starts to reorganize his or her life, adapts to the situation/event, and accepts reality.

Situational Crises and Coping Mechanisms

For many patients, a serious illness or injury constitutes a crisis. A crisis is the overwhelming events or series of events that create a situation perceived as threatening or unbearable. A situational crisis occurs when the unexpected event causes stress to a person or family, such as the development of an acute illness. The developmental stages of a crisis include:

- The person or family is in a state of homeostasis.
- The stressful event occurs
- Well-known coping skills fail to reduce the threat.
- A period of disequilibrium occurs.
- The problem is either resolved, or personal disintegration occurs.

A situational crisis is one where the problem leads to disruption of normal psychological functioning. Examples of situational crisis include an unwanted pregnancy, a new baby, divorce, death of a loved one, onset or change in a disease process, loss of job or career, and being a victim of a violent act. Community situational crises are events that affect an entire community. These include terrorist attacks, floods, hurricanes, earthquakes, and tornadoes.

Phases of a Crisis

- *Phase 1: External precipitating event* – There is a situation that occurs or something happens.

- *Phase 2: The threat* – A perceived or actual threat causes increased anxiety where the patient copes or fails to cope.

- *Phase 3: Failed coping* – The patient fails to cope, which produces physical symptoms, relationship problems, and increases disorganization.
- *Phase 4: Resolution* – There is mobilization of internal and external resources, and the patient is returned to the pre-crisis level of function.

Coping Mechanisms

Many patients respond to anxiety, stress, and crisis by using various coping skills that are learned over time. Coping mechanisms are learned external behaviors and internal thought processes that are used to decrease discomfort and pain. Coping behaviors can be emotion-focused or problem-focused. With emotion-focused behaviors, the patient alters a response to stress by thinking, saying or doing something that makes him or her feel happier or normal. These behaviors include crying, screaming, and talking with others. Problem-focused behaviors are done to alter the stressor in some way, such as investigating the facts of a problem or devising a plan to overcome the situation.

Self Defense Mechanisms

- *Denial* – Avoidance of a particular problem by refusing to recognize it or outright ignoring it.
- *Displacement* – Transfer of feelings for a threatening person, place, or thing to another neutral person, place, or thing.
- *Intellectualization* – Expressive thinking and logic adoption to avoid uncomfortable thoughts and feelings.
- *Projection* – Assignment of feelings or motivation to another person, place, or thing.
- *Rationalization* – Giving logical and acceptable explanations to hide a feeling, concern, or motive that is not socially acceptable.
- *Regression* – The demonstration of behavior characteristics that are from an earlier developmental stage.

Patient Assessment and Management

When arriving on the scene of a suspected behavior-related emergency, the EMS provider should size up the scene and determine the possible environmental dangers. Assess and observe the patient's demeanor, and check to see if he or she has any dangerous objects, such as a knife or gun. Also, attempt to ascertain whether or not the patient is under the effects of a chemical substance, such as drugs or alcohol.

Measures to Take

- Try to keep the patient calm by acting in a reassuring, respectful manner.

- Give the patient adequate space and be ready for sudden changes in behavior.

- Don't attempt to block the patient's means of exit.

- Don't interrupt or use a judgmental attitude.

- Don't leave the patient alone.

- Utilize soft restraints only when necessary.

- Be aware of the laws in your state concerning the use of restraints.

- For biting or spitting patients, apply a surgical or oxygen mask.

- Monitor the patient continuous for LOC, breathing, and circulation.

- Assess the patient's pulses, temperature, and skin color.

- Use law enforcement personnel when applicable.

Many patients will call EMS when going into labor for childbirth. Labor is the term used for the uterine contractions before giving birth. The three stages of labor include:

- *Moving the fetus into the birth canal* - The woman starts to feel contractions and the cervix dilates.

- *Fetus moves from the birth canal to the vagina* - After the cervix dilates to 10 cm, the fetus progresses to the vagina and the head will appear at the opening (crowning).

- Expelling the placenta - After the baby is born, the third stage of labor is when the mother expels the placenta.

Miscarriage

A miscarriage is a spontaneous abortion, in which the fetus is delivered but cannot survive or has died within the womb. This typically occurs during the first trimester (first three months) of pregnancy. Most women having a miscarriage experience pelvic cramping, heavy bleeding, and discharge of large clots or tissue.

If this occurs, the EMS provide should treat the woman's signs and symptoms, call for advanced life support (ALS) assistance, administer oxygen, apply vaginal pads to reduce or stop blood flow, and prepare for treatment of shock.

Preeclampsia and Eclampsia

During pregnancy, some women develop preeclampsia, which is a medical condition that causes the blood pressure to rise, as well as weight gain and water retention. When seizures occur, the woman is experiencing eclampsia, which is a medical emergency.

Trauma

If a pregnant woman experiences trauma, it could cause harm to the unborn fetus. The EMS provider should position the patient on her left side, administer oxygen, be prepared to treat shock and vomiting, and administer CPR in transport if necessary.

Emergency Delivery

EMT-B providers often have to perform a delivery when they arrive on the scene or when the patient is in transport to the hospital. Pre-delivery, the EMS provider should take proper body substance isolation precautions, determine what stage of labor the woman is in (hard = second stage), and examine her for bleeding or abnormal discharge.

Steps to Take

The delivery should occur with the patient lying on her back with her buttocks elevated by pillows. The steps include:

- When the baby crowns, press on the perineum to ensure the deliver does not occur too quickly.

- Avoid touching the fontanels (soft spots on the baby's head).

- As the baby presents outside of the body, remove the umbilical cord if it is around the neck.

- Place two clamps on the cord and cut it before removing it from the child's neck.

- Gently guide the head downward until the first shoulder blade emerges.

- Ensure that you have a secure hold on the infant and guide the infant upward for the second shoulder to pass.

- Maintain a firm grasp on the infant as the patient delivers the legs and feet.

- Give the baby to a team member to attend.

- Assist the mother in the final stage of labor, for placental delivery (may take 30 minutes or longer).

- Place the placenta in a plastic bag for the physicians to assess.

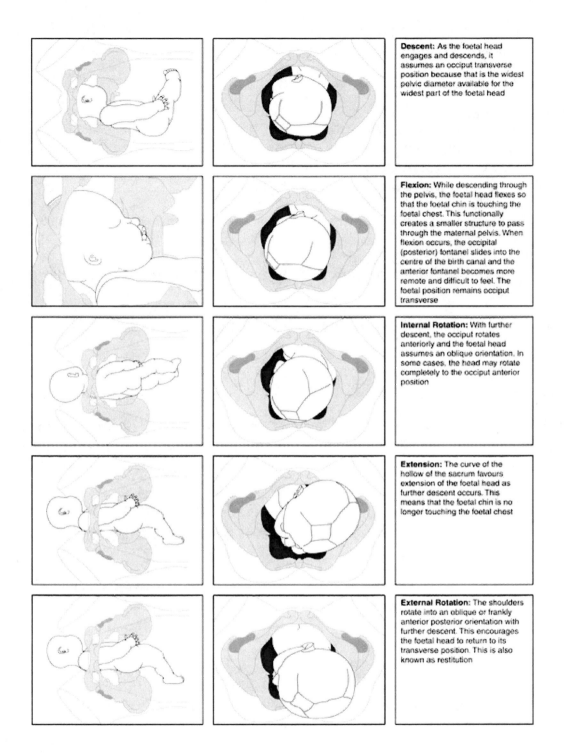

Descent: As the foetal head engages and descends, it assumes an occiput transverse position because that is the widest pelvic diameter available for the widest part of the foetal head

Flexion: While descending through the pelvis, the foetal head flexes so that the foetal chin is touching the foetal chest. This functionally creates a smaller structure to pass through the maternal pelvis. When flexion occurs, the occipital (posterior) fontanel slides into the centre of the birth canal and the anterior fontanel becomes more remote and difficult to feel. The foetal position remains occiput transverse

Internal Rotation: With further descent, the occiput rotates anteriorly and the foetal head assumes an oblique orientation. In some cases, the head may rotate completely to the occiput anterior position

Extension: The curve of the hollow of the sacrum favours extension of the foetal head as further descent occurs. This means that the foetal chin is no longer touching the foetal chest

External Rotation: The shoulders rotate into an oblique or frankly anterior posterior orientation with further descent. This encourages the foetal head to return to its transverse position. This is also known as restitution

Prolapsed Cord

A prolapsed cord is an infant condition where the umbilical cord appears out of the vagina first during the delivery. The cord will catch between the baby's head and the birth canal wall, and this will limit the baby's oxygen supply. Should this occur, elevate the patient's pelvic, administer high-flow oxygen, and direct her not to push.

145

Position fingers into the vagina and move the baby's head from the cord. Do not remove your hand until you reach the hospital.

Breech Presentation

When a baby presents feet first in the birth canal, it is called a breech presentation. This can lead to many emergencies, as the baby could suffocate if immediate action is not taken. To assist with a breech delivery, the EMT-B should:

- Place had in the vagina between the baby's face and the vaginal wall, making sure palm is up.

- Push the vaginal wall away from the infant's fact so oxygen can reach the head.

- Do not remove your hand until reaching the hospital.

Newborn Care

After the infant is delivered, The EMT-B must suction the nose and mouth to remove fluids, and then dry and swaddle the infant in a blanket or towel. Assessment of the infant includes:

- Check APGAR health at 1 minute and 5 minutes using scale.

- Assess newborn's appearance, activity level, grimace, pulse rate, and respirations.

- If not breathing, position and stimulate the infant as you assess airway, perform CPR, intubate, and administer drugs per protocol.

Sexual Assault

When EMS is called out regarding sexual assault, the patient may complain of pelvic pain and other injuries. To manage a sexual assault victim, the EMS provider should:

- Request law enforcement assistance.

- Avoid touching the patient without consent.

- Have a same-sex provider on the scene.

- Encourage the patient not to change clothes or take a shower.

- Treat clothing and personal items as evidence.

Trauma

- Recognize open wounds, amputations, blisters, impaled objects, closed wounds, wounds that require medical attention, and gunshot wounds.

- Describe first aid for a wounded victim.

- Identify reasons for the application of dressings and bandages.

- Describe first aid for burns.

- Recognize various types of burns: thermal burns, chemical burns, and electrocution.

- Describe burn care of first, second and third degree burns.

- Assess victim for head and brain injuries.

- Care for patients with head injuries, eye injuries, nosebleeds, dental injuries, or spine injuries.

- Recognize chest, abdominal, and pelvis injuries.

- Describe first aid for chest injuries: rib fractures, flail chest, impaled object in chest, and sucking chest wound.

- Describe first aid for abdominal injuries: blunt wound, penetrating wound, protruding organs.

- Describe first aid for pelvis injuries, extremity wounds, fractures.

- Recognize bone, joint, and muscle injuries.

- Describe first aid for joint injuries: dislocations, sprains.

- Explain first aid for muscle injuries: strains, contusions, cramps.

- Describe the effects of shock on the body's systems.

- Identify the signs and symptoms of shock.

Mechanisms of Injury

Trauma calls are the most difficult events for EMS providers. They often involve musculoskeletal damage, serious injuries, bleeding, shock, and soft tissue damage. The term mechanism of injury (MOI) is used to describe the manner of the trauma. Injuries can be blunt or penetrating, isolated or multisystem, high velocity or low velocity. Understanding the MOI will determine injury patterns, so the EMS can sharpen his or her index of suspicion.

Types of Motor Vehicle Collisions (MVC)

- *Head-on:* Vehicle occupants usually go up and over the steering wheel or down under the dash. Common injuries occur to the head, spine, chest, abdomen, hips, and lower extremities.

- *Rear impact:* These often result in cervical spine injury from hyperextension.

- *Lateral impact:* Often called the "T-bone," injuries occur along the side of the impact.

- *Rollover:* High risk of ejection and injury patterns are difficult to predict.

- *Rotational spins*: Increase the risk of cervical spine injury.

Patient Assessment and Management

Questions to ask bystanders and victims include:

- What speed was the vehicle going?

- What did the vehicle hit?

- Did the airbags deploy?

- Are the windows intact?

- What is the condition of the steering wheel, column, and dashboard?

Falls

The three aspects of assessment for a fall victim includes the distance fallen, the surface, and what part of the body was landed on.

Velocity Projectile Penetrating Injuries

- *Low-velocity*: Injury occurs along the path of the projectile, such as a knife, rebar, or pencil.

- *Medium-velocity*: The injury pattern is less predictable due to ricochet within the body, such as with a bullet from a handgun or rifle.

- *High-velocity*: The injury path is often many times larger than the projectile, due to formation of a space within the body from the projectile (cavitation). This occurs from assault with a rifle or gun.

Blast Injuries

- *Primary* - Injury is related to pressure wave of the blast.

- *Secondary* - Injury is related to flying debris.

- *Tertiary* - Injury is caused by being thrown against a stationary object.

- *Miscellaneous* - Injury is due to burn or inhalation.

Trauma Triage

High-priority trauma patients need to be transported to a Level 1 trauma center. The Centers for Disease Control and Prevention (CDC) lists the national trauma protocol on its website. The trauma center designations include:

- *Level 1* - Handles on-site trauma, surgery, intensive care, and rehabilitation.

- *Level 2* - Stabilizes trauma patients and transfers to a Level 1 center.

- *Levels 3 and 4* - Limited services available, so they stabilize and transfer patients.

Glasgow Coma Scale (GCS)

Eye Opening	Spontaneous	4
	To pain	3
	To speech	2
	None	1
Verbal Response	Alert and oriented	5
	Confused	4
	Incomprehensible	3
	Inappropriate	2
	None	1
Motor Response	Obeys commands	6
	Localizes pain	5
	Withdraws from pain	4
	Abnormal flexion	3
	Abnormal extension	2
	None	1
	Total Score	Min. 3 / Max. 5

Bleeding and shock are frequently encountered emergencies. Upon initial assessment, the EMT-B must determine where the patient is injured and how he or she should be treated. Internal bleeding is hard to recognize, just as the symptoms of shock are not always identifiable.

Compensated shock is the early stage of shock, and in this stage, the body can compensate through defense mechanisms. With decompensated shock (also known as late shock), there is progression of the condition, and the body can no longer compensate, so blood pressure and heart rate decreases. Finally, with irreversible shock, the final stage, the patient will not survive.

Types of Shock

There are several types of shock. The main causes of shock are heart pump problems (heart attack or trauma), blood volume issues (dehydration and bleeding, and pipe problems (anaphylaxis or spinal trauma).

Hypovolemic Shock

Shock occurs from an interruption in blood flow. Severe bleeding occurs and results in cell and organ damage as a direct result of decreased perfusion. This decrease in perfusion is known as hypoperfusion, which affects the entire body and leads to shock. With hypovolemic shock, there is inadequate blood volume and problems with the heart and vascular systems. Dehydration, severe vomiting and/or diarrhea, and blood loss are all causes of hypovolemic shock.

The signs and symptoms of hypovolemic shock include elevated heart rate, lowered blood pressure, altered breathing rate, weak thready pulses, shallow, or labored breathing, and pale, clammy skin. In the late stages when there is severe oxygen depletion, the patient may become combative, appear near death, and have very shallow irregular breathing.

Cardiogenic Shock

With cardiogenic shock, the heart muscle does not effectively pump blood and there is a backup of fluid and pulmonary edema. This results from low cardiac output and poor myocardial contractility. The symptoms and signs of cardiogenic shock are chest pain, respiratory distress, hypotension, pulmonary edema, and altered LOC.

Obstructive Shock

With obstructive shock, there is cardiac tamponade, where fluid accumulates in the pericardial sac and compresses the heart. The symptoms and signs include JVD, narrowing pulse pressures, hypotension and pale, clammy skin.

Distributive Shock

Also called pipe problem shock, distributive shock occurs due to widespread vasodilation. It can be related to relative hypovolemia or anaphylaxis. With an allergic reaction, there is bronchoconstriction, vasodilation, and vessel permeability (leakage). The signs and symptoms include hives, swelling, skin redness, weak pulses, hypotension, severe dyspnea, wheezing, and cyanosis.

Neurogenic Shock

Neurogenic shock occurs with spinal cord damage, and it leads to serious vasodilation below the level of injury. The symptoms and signs of this include hypotension, warm skin, paralysis, and respiratory paralysis.

Septic Shock

Septic shock is the result of severe infection, where blood vessels become damaged and there is increased plasma loss into the vascular space. This type of shock leads to hypovolemia, with symptoms of fever, chills, weakness, tachycardia, hypotension, cool clammy skin, weak pulses, and altered LOC.

Psychogenic Shock

Psychogenic shock often occurs from sudden, temporary vasodilation that leads to fainting. The sudden vasodilation interrupts the flow of blood to the brain, and a syncopal episode occurs.

Patient Assessment and Management

- Ensure the patient has a clear airway, especially for patients who are at risk for obstruction.

- Clear the airway, if necessary.

- Administer high-flow oxygen and allow for adequate ventilation.

- Manage and control bleeding (if applicable).

- Keep the patient warm to prevent loss of energy and oxygen.

- Prohibit patient movement.

- Elevate the legs to maximize blood flow to the brain.

External Bleeding

External bleeding can lead to shock if not controlled. Children, the elderly, and small patients have a lower blood volume and are particularly at risk. The three types of external bleeding are: arterial, venous, and capillary.

- *Arterial bleeding* - This occurs when an artery is damaged. Blood often spurts from the wound, and the patient can go into shock quickly. This type of bleeding is the most difficult to control.

- *Venous bleeding* - This starts from a vein, and is a lower pressure type of bleeding than the arterial form. Venous bleeding is easy to control.

- *Capillary bleeding* - With this type of bleeding, clots often form, making it easy to control.

Patient Assessment and Management

Bleeding is best controlled with concentrated direct pressure. This is done by using the fingertips to press on the wound with sterile gauze. For large wounds, diffuse direct pressure is necessary. With this method, the EMS provider must use sterile gauze pads to apply direct pressure using the entire hand. Other methods to control bleeding include:

- *Using pressure points* - This involves applying pressure on the area where the artery lies close to the bone. This reduces blood flow.

- *Splints* - When there are skeletal injuries, a splint will not only immobilize the bone injury, but decrease bleeding. This applies diffuse pressure to control bleeding while protecting blood vessels and tissues.

- *Tourniquets* - These are used as a last resort, because they pose a risk for permanent damage to nerves, blood vessels, and muscles. The tourniquet is applied to the area on the extremity above the wound.

- *Epistaxis* - Nasal bleeding occurs from blunt trauma or may arise spontaneously. To control this, place the patient in a seated, forward-leaning position, and pinch the nostrils together.

Internal Bleeding

Internal bleeding is difficult to identify and much harder to control than external bleeding. With internal blood loss, there is an increased risk for shock, so the EMS provider must recognize the symptoms and signs immediately. When organs are damaged, there may be bleeding from the mouth, anus, or genitals, and the patient could have pain, skin color changes, and swelling.

Patient Assessment and Management

- Maintain a patent airway.

- Administer supplemental oxygen.

- Rapidly transport patient to hospital.

- Use of anti-shock garment may be necessary.

There are basically three types of soft tissue injuries: open, closed, and burns. The skin has three layers. Soft tissue injuries often look worse than they actually are.

Open Injuries

Open injuries include breakage of the skin, and some external bleeding. These wounds are at risk for infection and should be covered with sterile dressings.

- *Abrasions* - Simple epidermal scrapes that result in mild pain, redness, and oozing blood.

- *Lacerations* - Cuts in the skin that can be linear (rectangular) or stellate (irregular). Most of these occur from forceful impact with sharp objects, such as broken glass or knives.

- *Puncture wounds* - Penetration occurs from a bullet or knife, and the wound may not bleed much.

- *Amputation* - Serious wound where the limb or appendage is severed from the body. With an amputation, expect massive bleeding.

Closed Injuries

Closed injuries have no external bleeding, and there are no open wounds. The three types are:

- *Contusions* - Bruises that are caused by blunt force to the skin, which damages blood vessels in the dermis.

- *Hematomas* - More severe forms of contusions. These result from damage to large blood vessels, and blood accumulates under the skin to form a bluish pooling.

- *Closed crush injuries* - When there is force applied to a body area from a blunt instrument, a crush injury can occur. These often result in internal bleeding.

Patient Assessment and Management

With most open or closed soft tissue injuries, it is best to first assess the patient for spinal injuries and immobilize if needed. Bleeding may be severe, especially with open injuries, so the patient must be monitored for signs of shock. Bleeding needs to be controlled per protocol, and the patient should be immediately transferred to the hospital. Wounds that require special treatment include:

- *Penetrating chest wound* - Must seal an occlusive dressing that won't allow air to enter or exit the wound.

- *Sucking chest wound* - Only seal the dressing on three sides to allow air to exit but not re-enter the wound.

- *Evisceration* - An abdominal injury where an organ is partially protruding outside of the body. The organ should be covered with a sterile dressing that has been moistened with sterile saline.

- *Foreign object* - When a foreign object is still in the wound, do not attempt to remove it, unless it interferes with the airway or CPR.

- *Amputation* - Wrap the salvageable appendage in plastic and keep it cool during transport.

- *Eye injury* - The eye may require flushing in some cases, but if an object is embedded, do not attempt to remove it. Cover both eyes with a sterile dressing.

Burns

Burns are painful injuries that may not be fatal, but can lead to compromise of the respiratory and circulatory systems. Burns may damage several layers of skin, so the patient is at risk for hypothermia, fluid loss, and infection. To assess the severity of burns, healthcare providers use what is known as the "Rule of Nines." Along with determining the severity of burns, this gives the EMS provider an idea of the patient's situation. Refer to the table on the following page to learn more about the Rule of Nines.

Rule of Nines

Area	Adults	Children	Infants
Head and neck	9%	12%	18%
Anterior trunk	18%	18%	18%
Posterior trunk	18%	18%	18%
Entire left leg	18%	16.5%	13.5%
Entire right leg	18%	16.5%	13.5%
Entire left arm	9%	9%	9%
Entire right arm	9%	9%	9%
Groin	1%	1%	1%
Total	100%	100%	100%

Burn Severity Depth

- *Superficial (first degree) burn* - Involves only the dermis, and is red and painful.

- *Partial thickness (second degree) burn* - Involves the epidermis and part of the dermis, and is painful with blistering.

- *Full thickness (third degree) burn* - Involves the dermal layer, and possibly the muscle and bone. Often has no pain, but the skin looks dry and leathery.

First-Degree Burns

First-degree burns involve superficial damage only, where the epidermis is slightly reddened and painful. Treatment involves the application of cool compress for pain relief and the prevention of infection with a dry sterile dressing.

Second-Degree Burns

Second-degree burns are called partial-thickness burns because they involve the epidermis, dermis, and some of the subcutaneous tissue. As with first-degree burns, the goal of treatment is to relieve pain and prevent infection. Cool the skin with cold water or a compress, and dress with a dry, sterile dressing.

Third-Degree Burns

Third-degree burns are called full-thickness burns, these injuries are the most serious of the three, involving all skin layers and some muscle and bone. If this occurs, cover the injured area with a sterile cloth and apply cool sterile water or normal saline. Keep the patient in a supine position with the head lower than the body. Remove any loose clothing or jewelry near the burn.

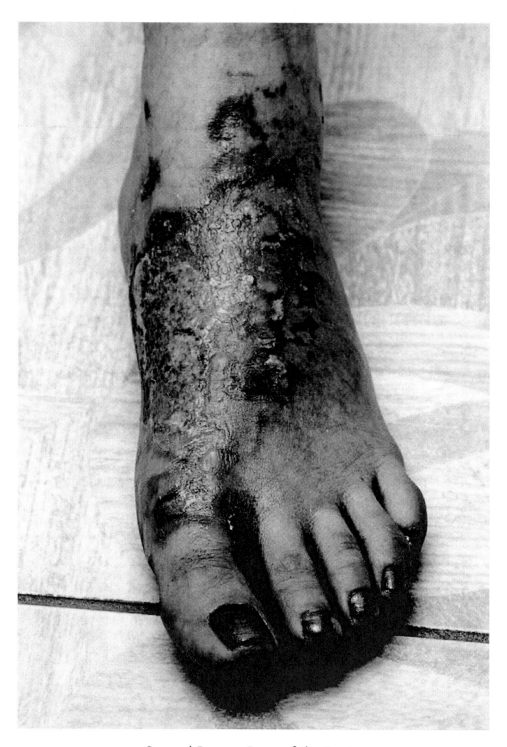

Second Degree Burn of the Foot

164

Thermal Burns

Thermal burns occur from heat, such as fire, water, or steam. With these burns, remove clothing that could trap heat and remove jewelry to prevent massive swelling. Stop the burning by using moist sterile burn sheets to the skin, and assess the patient for shock.

Chemical Burns

Chemical burns occur from exposure to a chemical substance. These may require the EMT-B to use PPE. The substance should be flushed away with water, and dry powder must be brushed away from the burned skin.

Electrical Burns

Electrical burns occur from an electrical source, and the patient is at high risk for cardiac arrest. With a victim, assess for entrance and exit wounds, and expect shock in these patients.

Patient Assessment and Management

- Keep the patient warm, as body temperature can drop.

- Do not cool large burns due to hypothermia risk.

- Airway burns can lead to swelling, so the patient may need oxygen.

Musculoskeletal Injuries

Musculoskeletal injuries are common in the EMS profession. The majority of these injuries do not require advanced or extensive treatment, but some can be life-threatening. In order to treat bone and joint injuries, the EMT-B must use the mechanism of injury and conduct a physical examination. Elderly patients are more at risk for skeletal injuries, due to osteoporosis and high risk for falls.

Fractures

Signs and symptoms of a fracture include pain, deformity, swelling, weak or absent pulses, and loss of function.

- *Open fracture* - An open fracture is associated with open soft tissue injury.
- *Closed fracture* - The skin is not broken.

Strains and Sprains

A strain is stretching of the muscle or tendon, which results in tenderness and pain. With a strain, there is little swelling and discoloration. A sprain is a ligament injury, often of the shoulder, knee, or ankle joints. The symptoms and signs include pain, tenderness, swelling, and discoloration of the skin (later).

Dislocation

A dislocation is when the bone moves out of normal joint position. The bone can be replaced into normal position by a doctor. The symptoms and signs of a dislocation include deformity, pain, weak or absent pulses, and loss of function.

Shoulder Dislocation

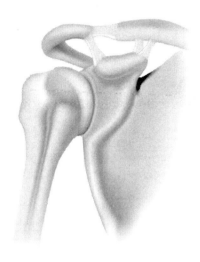 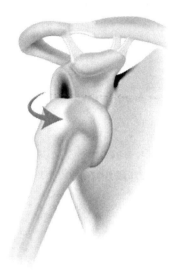 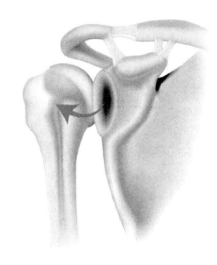

| Normal anatomy | Anterior dislocation | Posterior dislocation |

Potential Life-Threatening Injuries

- *Pelvic and hip fractures* - Older patients with a pelvic or hip fracture are at risk for embolism, pneumonia, hypovolemia, shock, and sepsis. The EMS provider should use splints to stabilize these and reduce bleeding.

- *Femur fractures* - Femur fractures are rare and can cause increased risk for embolism and hypovolemic shock.

Patient Assessment and Management

The main treatment for musculoskeletal injuries is splinting until the patient gets to the hospital. Splinting is done for most musculoskeletal injuries, and incorrect splint placement can lead to increased pain, compressed blood vessels, compromised circulation, and delayed transport. After applying the splint, assess distal pulse, motor, and sensation (PMS).

- *Pulse* - Assess pulse distal to the injury.

- *Motor* - Assess the ability to move the injured extremity.

- *Sensation* - Assess the ability to sense touch below the injury area.

Types of Splints

- *Rigid splints* - These are non-formable splints that support an injured extremity and immobilize surrounding bones and joints.

- *Traction splints* - These splints are flexible and conform to the wound.

- *Air splint* - The wound must first be covered with clean dressings and then covered with an air splint.

- *Pneumatic anti-shock garments* - These are used to immobilize lower extremities when the patient has a femur, hip, or pelvic fracture or serious injury to the lower region.

- *Vacuum splints* - Used to place the injured extremity in an inflated device so the vacuum removes air and the splint conforms to the extremity.

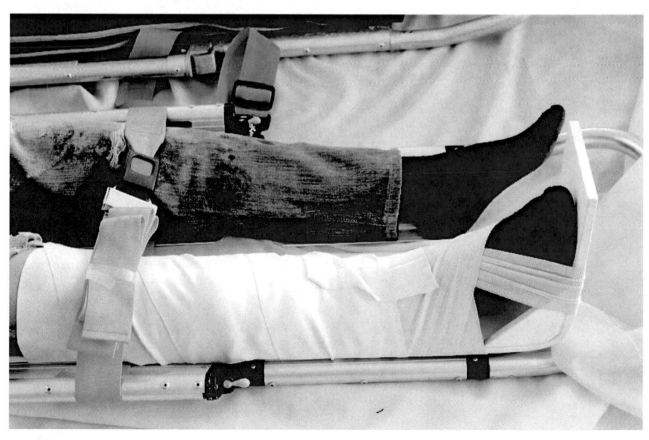

Injuries to the Head, Brain, and Spine

Injuries to the head, brain, and skull often are accompanied by spinal cord trauma. Any patient with a suspected head injury should be fully immobilized for this reason. Head, brain, and spine injuries are quite dangerous, as they require extremely careful assessment and immobilization on arrival to the trauma scene. Rapid transport to the medical center is important with these types of injuries because of the potential life-threatening consequences.

Scalp Injuries

Scalp injuries are either open or closed. Most of these will require sutures for repair. The scalp bleeds profusely, as it is highly vascular. Scalp wounds often appear worse than they accurately are.

Skull Fractures

Skull fractures occur when there is an actual break to one of the skull bones. They often indicate a potential brain injury. Types of skull fractures include:

- *Linear fracture* - The fracture is linear, does not present with a deformity, and has no depression.

- *Depressed fracture* - The fracture is depressed and noticeable with palpation. This type of fracture puts the patient at risk for brain damage due to displacement of bone into the actual brain tissue.

- *Basal fracture* - Often called a basilar skull fracture, these occur at the base of the skull. Cerebrospinal fluid often will leak from the ears and/or nose with this type of fracture. Indicators of this fracture are Battle's sign (bruising behind ears) and raccoon eyes (bruising under eyes).

Brain Injuries

- *Concussion* - A concussion is brain trauma that results when the brain is hit in a blunt manner. Symptoms and signs often occur rapidly, and include altered LOC, brief LOC, nausea, vomiting, vision problems, amnesia, and irritability. These will typically improve gradually.

- *Cerebral contusion* - A cerebral contusion usually occurs along with edema or a concussion. The signs and symptoms include decreased mental status, changes in vital signs, pupillary changes, and behavioral abnormalities.

- *Epidural hematoma* - This is when bleeding occurs beneath the skull and above the dura mater. It is an extremely dangerous condition, and is often seen with a temporal skull fracture. Symptoms and signs include altered LOC, seizures, headache, posturing, hypertension, vomiting, pupillary changes, and bradycardia.

- *Subdural hematoma* - this refers to bleeding above the brain, just beneath the dura mater and above the arachnoid meningeal layer. This type of bleeding often follows a cerebral contusion. Signs and symptoms include vomiting, decreasing LOC, weakness, paralysis, headache, seizures, hypertension, pupillary changes, and altered respirations.

- *Subarachnoid hemorrhage* - This type of bleeding occurs within the subarachnoid space, and the injury allows the blood to enter the cerebrospinal fluid (CSF). It can be due to trauma or a ruptured aneurysm, and symptoms include stiff neck, headache, decreased LOC, and seizures.

- *Intracerebral hemorrhage* - Bleeding within the brain tissue that leads to an increased risk of death.

- *Herniation syndrome* - Herniation of the brain occurs when there is compression due to excessive intracranial pressure (ICP). Signs of increased ICP include hypertension, bradycardia, and changes in breathing.

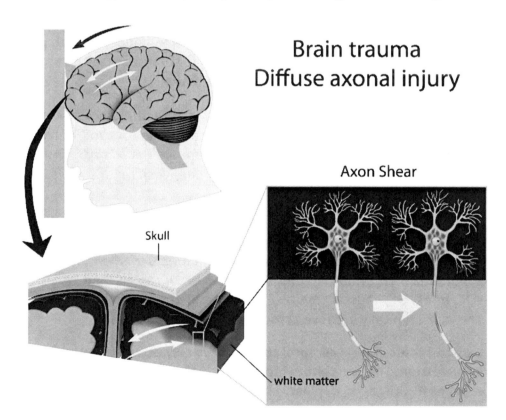

Brain trauma
Diffuse axonal injury

Axon Shear

Skull

white matter

Spinal Injuries

Mechanism of Injury

- *Flexion* - Extreme forward movement of the head (chin to chest)

- *Extension* - Extreme backward movement of the head (rear-impact accident).

- *Rotation* - Extreme lateral movement (side to side).

- *Compression* - Head compressed against the body (diving injury).

- *Distraction* - Stretching of the spinal column and cord (hanging).

- *Penetration* - Injury from a stab or gunshot wound.

- *Lateral bending* - Extreme bending of the head to one side (ear to shoulder).

Signs and Symptoms

- *Pain or tenderness*

- *Motor deficits* - Weak or absent grips, inability to push or pull

- *Sensory deficits* - Inability to feel or sense touch

- *Paraplegia* - Paralysis of the lower extremities

- *Quadriplegia* - Paralysis of all extremities

Transected Cord

A transected cord is where the spinal cord is severed, and there is paralysis below the level of injury. With this type of trauma, there is loss of bowel and/or bladder control, possible respiratory arrest, and high risk of mortality.

Neurogenic Shock

Neurogenic shock occurs with spinal cord injury. Symptoms and signs of this include hypotension, priapism (involuntary penile erection), loss of bladder/bowel control, and paralysis below the level of injury.

Spinal Immobilization

With an injury to the head, brain, or spinal column, the EMS providers will need to provide spinal immobilization to the victim. Manual cervical spine precautions should be taken. The long spine board is used for supine or standing patients, and is often needed due to potential problems related to airway, breathing, and/or circulation. A half spine board can be used for patients needing to be removed from a vehicle.

Patient Assessment and Management

- Use DCAP-BTLS to assess injuries.

- Secure an airway, and ventilate if necessary.

- Control bleeding.

- Be prepared for rolling the patient to the left side if vomiting occurs.

- Use a cervical collar when spinal trauma is evident.

- Use rolled up blankets for immobilization if needed to keep the head in a neutral position.

- Immobilize the spine with a half board or long spine board.

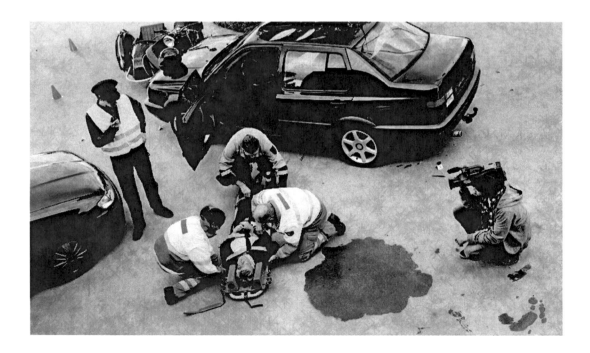

Foreign Objects in the Eye

When objects do not penetrate the eye, they can easily be removed by irrigating. Symptoms include pain, scratchy sensation, and tearing. Most EMS protocols only allow for eye irrigation for chemical burns and irritants.

Corneal Abrasion

The cornea is the transparent covering of the iris (colored eye portion). When there is trauma to this, abrasion is likely. Symptoms include pain, scratchy sensation, and tearing.

Orbital Fracture

When there is head and spinal trauma, an orbital fracture could occur. The symptoms of this are deformity around the eye orbit, visual disturbances, double vision, loss of sensation, and inability to move the eye upward.

Chemical Burns of the Eye

With chemicals entering the eyes, the EMT-B needs to do immediate and continuous irrigation. Care should be taken to avoid irrigating the chemical substance into the other eye.

Impaled Objects in the Eye

With an impaled object in the eyeball, do not remove the object. Instead, stabilize the patient and encourage him or her to keep both eyes closed to prevent movement of the object.

Loss of Tooth

If you respond to a call regarding dislodgement and loss of a permanent tooth, control the bleeding with sterile gauze. Also, rinse the tooth with sterile saline and transport it to the facility in saline-soaked gauze.

Nasal Injuries

For suspected nasal fractures, apply cold compresses. Never pack the nares, however, but control bleeding per local protocol. Avoid putting the patient in the supine position, as this could compromise the airway.

Ear Injuries

Apply direct pressure to the ear to control any bleeding. If any tissue emerges from the ear canal or is severed from the ear itself, preserve that in saline-soaked gauze. Do not pack the ear canal.

Neck Trauma

If a patient sustains an injury of the neck, the EMS provider's priority is to secure the airway. Also, any life-threatening bleeding must be controlled with pressure. Apply an occlusive dressing to any large open neck wounds, to reduce any risk of an air embolism.

Chest Injuries

Chest injuries occur as a result of penetrating or blunt trauma. The signs and symptoms of a chest injury include tenderness, bruising, obvious penetrating wound, paradoxical motion, respiratory distress, hemoptysis (coughing up blood), hypoxia, JVD, abnormal lung sounds, and shock.

Types of Chest injuries

- *Pneumothorax* - This is when air accumulates in the lung's pleural space, resulting in compression of the lung space. A pneumothorax prevents gas exchange, results in hypoxia, and can be unrelated to trauma. Symptoms and signs include chest pain, dyspnea, and diminished lung sounds.

- *Sucking chest wound* - Also called an open pneumothorax, this is an open chest injury that penetrates the pleural space. The wound will draw air during inhalation, so it should be covered with a three-sided occlusive dressing.

- *Hemothorax* - When there is bleeding into the pleural space, a hemothorax occurs. The symptoms of this are chest pain, dyspnea, and shock.

- *Cardiac tamponade* - This occurs when fluid and/or blood accumulates in the sac around the heart (pericardial sac), and the pressure from this compresses the heart. Assess for Beck's triad: JVD, muffled heart sounds, and narrowing pulse pressure.

Rib and Clavicle Fractures

Clavicle and rib fractures are often associated with a pneumothorax. These are common occurrences. The patient may present with subcutaneous emphysema, which is a crackling sensation of the skin caused by air escaping into the subcutaneous tissue.

Flail chest occurs when a part of the thorax is separated from the other portion of the thorax. Flail chest is caused by a fracture of at least two consecutive ribs in two places or more than that. It often occurs when the sternum gets separated from the rib cage.

Patient Assessment and Management

- Scene size-up to assure safe environment.

- BSI with eye and face protection.

- Analyze MOI to determine if there is an open or closed injury.

- Assess respiratory and circulatory effort.

- Maintain open airway.

- Establish cervical immobilization.

- Provide oxygen at 15 L/minute or per protocol.

- Provide stabilization of an impaled object.

- Closely monitor for shock, and treat if appropriate with warmth and positioning.

Abdominal Injuries

Abdominal injury occurs when there is damage to solid organs of the abdomen. This puts the patient at risk for hemorrhagic shock, as these organs can bleed profusely. The spleen, liver, kidneys, pancreas, stomach, intestines, and urinary bladder all can spill their contents when injured. Symptoms and signs of an abdominal injury vary, but include pain in the shoulder, bruising, distension, pain, tenderness, guarding, and shock.

Patient Assessment and Management

- Determine priority status.

- Maintain appropriate spinal protection.

- Maintain an open airway.

- Give high-flow oxygen at 15 L/minute.

- With abdominal evisceration, when there is significant trauma to the abdominal tissue, do not attempt to replace the organ or tissue.

- Cute away clothing from the wound.

- Apply a pre-moistened dressing over the area.

- Apply an occlusive dressing over the moist dressing.

- Control any bleeding.

- Position the patient supine with legs flexed at the knees.

Treating Infants and Children

Learning Objectives

- Recognize the developmental differences in pediatric patients.

- Explain how to handle airway obstructions in infants and children.

- Identify and treat various pediatric illnesses and injuries.

- Understand the pediatric assessment triangle.

With infants, the tongue is proportionally larger than adults, which allows little room for swelling. The pediatric lower airway is small, and is more easily obstructed than the adult's. A child's head is also proportionally larger in relation to the body than compared to that of an adult. Infants and children are at increased risk for head trauma.

Developmental Differences

Newborns and Infants (Birth to 12 Months)

- Minimal stranger anxiety.

- Should be kept warm.

- Assess breathing rate from a distance (often abdominal breathing).

Toddlers (1 to 3 Years)

- Do not like to be separated from parents.

- Do not like to be touched or examined.

- Afraid of needles and pain.

- Should be examined trunk to head to establish trust.

Preschool (3 to 6 Years)

- Do not like to be touched.

- Does not like being separated from parents.

- Afraid of blood and pain.

- Fears permanent injury.

- Extremely modest.

School Age (6 to 12 Years)

- Afraid of blood and pain.

- Fears permanent injury and disfigurement.

- Modest.

Adolescent (12 to 18 Years)

- Fear of disfigurement and permanent injury.

- May desire to be checked away from the parents.

- Modest and prideful.

One of the most common reasons for EMS to respond to a call regarding an infant or child is an airway obstruction. A partial obstruction is when the child is awake, but agitated and distressed. Most of these patients can remove the object without assistance. A complete obstruction involves an altered mental status, changes in skin tone and color, and inability to cry or speak.

Removal of Obstructions - Infant

- Position the infant so he or she is face down.

- Deliver five back blows between the shoulders.

- Turn the infant face up and assess for the object.

- If not seen, deliver five chest thrust over the lower half of the sternum.

- Repeat this until the airway is unobstructed or the child becomes responsive.

Removal of Obstructions - Child

- Place the child in the supine position.

- Look for the obstructed object by performing the tongue jaw lift.

- When you spot the object, remove with a finger sweep.

- Open the airway and assess for breathing.

- If not breathing, attempt to ventilate.

- Begin chest compressions.

- Reassess for the foreign body.

Fontanel Abnormalities

A sunken fontanel in an infant could indicate dehydration or hypovolemia. A bulging fontanel is an indication of increased intracranial pressure. Children require more blood flow to the brain, so hypoxia can occur rapidly.

Chest Injuries

Children's ribs are pliable, so there is a decreased risk of rib fractures but an increased risk for internal injury. Also, children have lower tidal volumes of the lungs, so there is an increased risk of over-inflation.

Sudden Infant Death Syndrome (SIDS)

Sudden infant death syndrome is the unexpected death of an infant that cannot be attributed to a cause. SIDS is only confirmed on autopsy. The EMS provider should attempt to revive the infant and provide emotional support to the parents.

Croup

Croup refers to a respiratory condition that affects infants and young children. The symptoms and signs include barking couth, stridor, hoarseness, and difficulty breathing. The Estly score system designates mild croup as barking cough and hoarseness but no stridor. With moderate and sever croup, there will be serious distress and stridor.

Altered Mental Status

In pediatric patients, an altered mental status can occur from poisoning, head trauma, infection, hypoglycemia, infection, head trauma, hypoperfusion, and decreased oxygen levels.

Shock

For children and infants, shock occurs from trauma, blood loss, infection, diarrhea, dehydration, vomiting, and abdominal injuries. The signs and symptoms include rapid breathing, pale and clammy skin, weak or absent pulses, decreased capillary refill, mental status changes, absence of tearing, and decreased urine output.

Pediatric Assessment Triangle (PAT)

The pediatric assessment triangle (PAT) includes appearance, breathing, and circulation.

Appearance - Tone, Interactivity, Consolability, Look, and Speech (TICLS)

- *Tone* - Assess for muscle tone and movement.

- *Interactivity* - Assess for reactivity to stimulus, alertness, and environmental interaction.

- *Consolability* - Assess if the child is able to be consoled.

- *Look* - Determine if the child can fix his or her gaze.

- *Speech* - Assess the speech or cry of the child for strength and quality.

Breathing

Any problems with respirations and breathing effort could indicate a serious respiratory system problem. Assess for how hard the child must work to breathe, examining for use of accessory muscles, grunting, head bobbing, abnormal lung sounds, and nasal flaring.

Circulation

The circulation to skin is often a determining factor for serious injury. Abnormal findings indicate shock or a cardiac issue. Look for pale skin, cyanosis, mottled or flushed appearance, and/or jaundice.

Patient Assessment and Management

- Use padding behind the shoulders to immobilize the pediatric patient in an in-line, neutral position.

- Perform the pediatric assessment triangle (PAT).

- Bradycardia should be treated as a sign of hypoxia.

- Administer artificial ventilation and suction if necessary.

- Keep the patient warm

- Elevate legs if shock is evident.

- Manage bleeding if applicable.

Operations

Learning Objectives

- Identify various ambulance operations.

- Explain infection control procedures, aseptic measures, and safety techniques.

- Understand the purpose of equipment management.

- Identify measures for scene safety, access, extrication.

- Understand how to handle hazardous materials emergencies

- Explain multiple casualty incidents and what to do in the event of a mass casualty.

Ambulance and Air Medical Operations

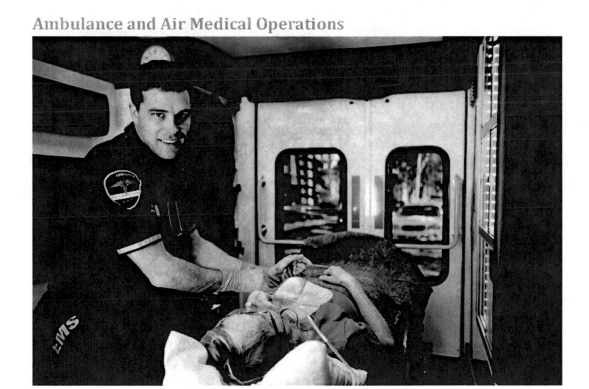

Ambulance Design

A modern ambulance meets certain criteria:

- Separate compartments for the driver and the patient.

- Room for at least two EMS providers and two patients.

- Compliant with local, state, and federal safety and certification requirements.

- Has all necessary medical equipment for the scope of practice given.

- Radio communication with dispatchers.

- Connection to online medical direction.

Types of Ambulances

- *Type I* – Truck chassis with modular ambulance body.

- *Type II* – Standard van design.

- *Type III* – Specialty van design with a square patient compartment mounted on the chassis.

Ambulance Call Phases

- *Preparation phase* – Inspect the ambulance after shift change each day.

- *Dispatch* – Determine the nature of the call, the number of victims, and the location.

- *En route to scene* – Notify the dispatch that you are responding, and operate according to all state and local laws and agency rules and regulations.

- *Arrival on the scene* – Notify dispatch when you reach the scene, and position the ambulance to allow for safe egress and patient loading.

- *While on the scene* – Use the ambulance as a barrier to protect the scene.

- *Patient transfer* – The patient is to be properly secured for transport, and notify dispatch that you are en route.

- *Arrival at hospital* – Notify dispatch you have arrived, provide a verbal report to hospital personnel, give a copy of written patient care record, and obtain appropriate signatures.

- *Post-run phase* – Restock and return all equipment to be ready for the next call, and clean/disinfect/sterilize per agency protocol.

Defensive Driving Techniques

- Quality of care overrides speed of response, so do not sacrifice patient safety for quick transport.

- Everyone should be adequately restrained in the vehicle during transport, as well as all equipment.

- The emergency vehicle needs to be in the far left lane.

- The driver should always know what is next to him or her.

- Scan the road frequently.

- Anticipate unexpected actions from other drivers.

- Always assume that other drivers do not see you.

- Pass on the left if necessary.

- Remember that you have blind spots and minimize them.

- Use daytime running lights according to local protocol.

- Recognize that ambulances have a high center of gravity, so take corners carefully.

- Use lights and sirens together.

- Recognize fatigue as a serious threat to vehicle operation.

Air Transport Ambulances

Air ambulances are helicopters that have rotor-wings, or they can be planes, with fixed-wings. The landing zone is the secure area where the aircraft must land, and should be completely clear. Be sure to remove loose debris, and assure a firm, level surface. The takeoff and landing are the two most dangerous aspects of air transport flight. Additionally, there needs to be constant radio contact between the pilot of the air ambulance and someone on the ground who is giving critical information during landing, approach, and takeoff.

Never approach the air ambulance without permission, and always approach from the front. Make sure that all loose items are secured before attempting to approach the aircraft to load the patient. Be familiar with local protocols that are related to air medical operations. Not all patients should be transferred via the air route.

EMS providers have to responds to calls where the patient is trapped inside a vehicle. For these events, the personal safety of the EMT-B is paramount. It will be difficult to assist anyone if you are injured. Rescue operations are often handed by specially trained rescue personnel, firefighters, and police officers. Some EMS agencies will require the EMT-B to take special courses regarding rescue operation techniques, so they will be able to assist with certain emergencies.

Extrication

Extrication is the term for the process where the patient is removed from a vehicle or any other dangerous situation. In many incidences, you must remove objects and debris from the area first, which is called disentanglement. Specialized equipment may be necessary for this process.

Hydraulic extrication tools are used mainly by firefighters to extricate the patient. When these are used, the rescue crew must wear protective gear, such as goggles and helmets. In trauma situations, EMS providers should implement cervical spine precautions, control bleeding, manage the airway, and supply oxygen to the patient.

Safety and Equipment

During a rescue, safety should be the primary EMS concern. The EMT-B needs to ensure his/her safety, as well as the safety of the partner, the patient(s), and any bystanders. This is done before attempting to assess or treat any victims.

- *EMT-B Safety:* This is best done by wearing protective gear appropriate for the emergency, such as a helmet, leather gloves, and goggles. Most EMS providers wear puncture-resistant clothing and steel-toed boots for specific incidents.

- *Patient Safety:* Once on the scene, EMS provider need to make sure the patient(s) are protected from further harm, which includes removing them from dangerous debris, such as metal and glass. Use a blanket to cover the victim as you remove him or her from the scene.

- *Vehicle Safety:* One main risk at the scene is a fire of the motor vehicle. Be sure to turn the vehicle's engine off, and move that patient far away from the vehicle if it is on fire.

- *Electric Shock*: A downed power line should only be handled by utility workers with special training. Don't approach the line. Get help from authorities before attempting to treat the patient.

- *Hazardous Materials*: The safety officer will oversee the removal of hazardous materials. This person observes the scene and notes any potential hazards that could harm the rescue personnel during the emergency.

Fire Safety Measures

Although rare, fires in physician offices do occur. The medical assistant should be aware of certain fire safety measures, including:

- Keep open spaces free of clutter.

- Mark fire exits.

- Know the locations of fire exits, alarms, and extinguishers.

- Know the fire drill and evacuation plan of the healthcare facility.

- Don't use the elevator when a fire occurs.

- Turn off oxygen in the vicinity of the fire.

Electrical Safety Measures

Before use, electrical equipment should be inspected for defects and safety. This involves the use of three-pronged outlets and reading warning labels. Any electrical cords that are exposed, damaged, or frayed should be discarded, and circuits should not be overloaded. Safety measures include:

- Never run electrical wiring under carpets.

- Don't pull a plug by using the cord.

- Never use electrical appliances near bathtubs, sinks, or other water sources.

- Disconnect a plug from the outlet before cleaning appliances or equipment.

- Never operate unfamiliar equipment.

Radiation Safety Measures

Radiation safety involves the use of various protocols and guidelines of the healthcare facility. Radiation exposure is monitored with a film badge. Safety measures include:

- Label potentially radioactive material.

- Limit time spent near the source.

- Use a shielding device to protect vital organs.

- Place the patient with radiation implants in private room.

Accessing and Removing the Patient

Simple access to the patient will not require any special equipment or training. If a motor vehicle is involved, the EMS provider must wear protective clothing. Never attempt to access the patient without special extrication training.
Once the EMT-B gains access to the patient, he or she should assist with extrication. If a spinal injury is suspected, the patient's spine must be stabilized before he or she is moved. If there is immediate danger, do not wait to stabilize the spine, however.

To serve on the special response team, the EMT-B needs additional training. The more educated the provider in disaster response, the more prepared he or she is for a mass-casualty emergency or situation that involves hazardous materials.

Hazardous Material

Most agencies and local regulations require the EMT-B to complete a First Responder Awareness Level education program before handling hazardous materials situations. These materials pose serious threats to people's lives: bystanders, patients, and EMS providers. The hazardous materials handling programs will assure that you understand the EMS role in the response plan, recognize the presence of hazardous materials and their risks, and understand outcomes of these situations.

Approaching the Scene

The first measure when approaching the scene is to isolate and avoid the area where the hazardous material is located. This involves recognizes sounds, clouds, or odors that indicate the presence of hazardous materials. When doing this, it is vital that you report anything unusual to dispatch.

Sources of Information

Material Safety Data Sheets (MSDS) are electronic or hard copy papers that explain detains about the substance or chemical. The U.S. Department of Labor requires organizations to keep these as public records for all chemicals used. This information will help EMS providers to deal with hazardous materials. Place the material in a container when found, making sure it is noted if the chemical is flammable, radioactive, or corrosive.

Emergency Procedures

Many EMS agencies use the Emergency Response Guidebook, which is a manual device to help those who work with hazardous materials. During the emergency procedure, the provider must:

- Use caution when approaching the scene

- Make sure he or she is wearing appropriate protective gear

- Identify hazardous materials and their sources

- Follow the guidelines in the Guidebook

- Don't allow anyone to enter a contaminated zone

- Call CHEMTREC for directions or the medical director

- Isolate any patients who have been contaminated by the toxin.

- Avoid puddles, clouts, or spilled materials

- Do not inhale any vapors, fumes, or smoke

Incident Management Systems

Local and state organizations create incident management systems to ensure efficient and effective responses by police and fire departments, as well as EMS crews. These systems will help the crew members understand their responsibilities. These systems are used in situations involving multiple extrications or hazardous materials.

Sectors

There are several designated sectors involved, once a major incident is declared. These include:

- *Staging sectors* – Responsible for movement of all transportation vehicles that arrive and leave the scene.

- *Transportation sector* – Involves the use of helicopters and ambulances to transport personnel, patients, and equipment.

- *Support sector* – Request receipts for supplies and support services and coordinates with the transportation center.

- *Extrication sector* – Responsible for removing trapped patients.

- *Treatment sector* – Receives the patients from various sectors and prioritizes them for transport.

- *Triage sector* – Responsible for the continued reassessment and further treatment of patients.

Mass-Casualty Situations

During mass-casualty situations, the incident management system will organize and direct emergency workers. Some examples of these events include train collisions, explosions, building collapses, and earthquakes.

Patient Prioritizing

During a mass-casualty situation, the EMT will perform patient triage. The triage method is a form of categorizing patients according to injury severity. A tagging system is used to indicate which patients require immediate treatment. The color-coded or numbered tags indicate:

- *Life-threatening* – Require immediate transport.

- *Moderate* – Require transport as soon as possible.

- *Minor* – Require delayed transport.

- *Not injured* – No transport required.

- *Deceased* – No transport necessary.

A tactical emergency medical support (TEMS) team may be called in to deal directly with anyone involved in a threatening situation. This crew involves EMS personnel who are specifically trained to handle traumatic events.

TEMS Responsibilities

The TEMS members must be ready to encounter and treat certain conditions:

- Gunshot wounds

- Tear gas or pepper spray exposure

- Cardiac or respiratory arrest

- Penetrating trauma

- Heat stroke

- Hypothermia

- Explosion injuries

- Chemical burns

- Hazardous material exposure

Field Care and Triage

The tactical leader and the team members create three zones: the cold zone, the warm zone, and the hot zone.

- *Cold zone* – This is where EMS workers and patients are both safe from any future threats.

- *Warm zone* – The outer perimeter of the scene, where contact with perpetrators is not likely.

- *Hot zone* – The inner perimeter where there is a persistent or unknown threat.

TEMS providers and BLS providers first size up the scene. The scene assessment involves the ACE method, which stands for assessment, cover and concealment, and evacuation. The TEMS providers consider the risks that could occur for bystanders, patients, and themselves.

Zone Assignment

The level of care provided to the patient will depend on the zone he or she is assigned. In the hot zone, the perpetrator or threat may still be lingering, so it is vital to ensure the safety of the patient as well as emergency personnel. Not many medical interventions are performed in the hot zone.

In the warm zone, there is a safe distance from the threat, so workers can perform CPR and other life saving measures. Steps to take include:

- If the patient has a weapon, disarm him or her.

- Assess airway, breathing, and circulation.

- Position the patient in the recovery position.

- Inspect the patient for additional injuries such as those from contact with hazardous materials.

- Splint any fractures and immobilize the spine if necessary.

In the cold zone, the patient is no longer at risk of injury or contamination. The ALS providers will tend to serious injuries in this zone before patient transport. Minor injuries are also treated in the cold zone, such as abrasions and minor wounds.

Weapons of Mass Destruction

Weapons of mass destruction (WMD) present unique challenges for EMS workers from three distinct sources: international terrorist, domestic issue terrorists, and lone terrorists. EMS crews often are the first persons on the scene of a WMD incident.

Chemical Substances

There are many common chemical agents used in mass terrorism. These agents cause cholinergic crisis, a toxin condition. To identify symptoms related to a cholinergic crisis, the EMS provider can use the SLUDGEM method to assess patients.

Nerve Agents

Nerve agents are a significant threat due to the ease of use and how simple they are to acquire. These agents cause excessive parasympathetic nervous system stimulation, and include Tabun, Soman, VX, and Sarin. If a patient is exposed to a nerve agent, the EMS provider must use aggressive airway management, which includes suction and support by ventilation. The patient may require certain medications to counteract the nerve agent's effects.

Vesicants

Vesicants can lead to blistering, pain, and burns to the skin, respiratory tract, and eyes. Also called blistering agents, these agents have a delayed onset of action, and affected areas should be irrigated with large amounts of water as soon as exposure occurs.

Cyanide

Cyanide is a substance that interferes with the body's ability to deliver oxygen to the cells, and this often leads to hypoxia and death. Known as a blood agent, cyanide symptoms and signs include weakness, dizziness, anxiety, tachypnea, nausea, seizures, and respiratory arrest. The management of a patient exposed to cyanide includes administration of high-flow oxygen, support with positive-pressure ventilation, and antidotes for the poisoning, which can be given by ALS personnel.

Pulmonary Agents

Also referred to as choking agents, pulmonary agents cause lung damage. The symptoms and signs of these include dyspnea, wheezing, runny nose, cough, and sore throat. Management of these agents includes maintaining the airway, giving the patient oxygen as needed, and ventilation support.

Biological Agents

Biological agents are used to inflict disease upon the victims. The signs and symptoms vary, but typically include fever, chills, respiratory distress, and a flu-like illness. Management of the patient includes supportive care related to the symptoms.

Nuclear and Radiological Weapons

Nuclear weapons can result in death from a blast, thermal burns, or radiation. Nuclear radiation can kill humans and other living things, and it also causes birth defects and cancer.

- *Alpha radiation* – This form can only travel short distances, and is a dense, slow-moving substance. It is stopped by the skin, clothing, and outerwear, but can be dangerous if ingested or inhaled.

- *Beta radiation* – This type is slow-moving, but can penetrate the first few millimeters of the skin. Serious risks of exposure occur when the patient is contaminated by inhalation or ingestion.

- *Gamma radiation* – Also called X-ray radiation, this type can travel long distances, and easily penetrates the body. External hazard can occur with exposure.

Radiation Exposure

Signs and symptoms of radiation include nausea, vomiting, diarrhea, headache, fever, and skin lesions. Protection from this involves TDS (time, distance, and shielding).

- Time – Don't spend time around it.

- Distance – Stay as far from it as possible.

- Shielding – Required to block the radiation.

Management

If you are concerned a victim has been exposed to radiation, the clothing and skin are likely contaminated. Also, all body fluids should be considered contaminated, as well. The patient must be removed from the area, and treated for acute injuries before transfer to the hospital. During treatment, the EMS providers should wear protective clothing and shielding devices.

Practice Examination

1. **The pulse in the foot is called the:**

A. Carotid
B. Radial
C. Femoral
D. Dorsalis pedis

Answer: D. Dorsalis pedis

Explanation: The carotid pulse is along the neck, the radial pulse is found at the wrist, the femoral pulse is located at the groin, and the pedal pulse (foot) is called the dorsalis pedis.

2. **The midline of the body is called the:**

A. Middle
B. Lateral
C. Medial
D. Side

Answer: C. Medial

Explanation: The lateral aspect of the body is the sides. The medial aspect is the midline of the body.

3. **Which organization increased awareness of cardiovascular prevention in the 1980s?**

A. The American Medical Association (AMA)
B. The American Nurses Association (ANA)
C. The American Heart Association (AHA)
D. The U.S. Heart Association (USHA)

Answer: C. The American Heart Association (AHA)

Explanation: In the 1980s, the American Heart Association (AHA) increased awareness of cardiovascular disease prevention, and additional EMS levels of training were added to accommodate this.

4. **Which are the current national standard curricula for emergency medical technicians?**

A. The National EMS Education Standards (NEMSES)
B. The National Registry of Emergency Medical Technicians (NREMT)
C. The National Highway Transportation Safety Administration (NHTSA)
D. The Emergency Responders Standards (ERS)

Answer: A. The National Registry of Emergency Medical Technicians (NREMT)

Explanation: In the 1990s, the National Registry of Emergency Medical Technicians (NREMT) advocated national training for EMS providers, and the National Highway Transportation Safety Administration (NHTSA) started the *EMS Agenda for the Future* document. In the 2000s, the NHTSA replaces standard curricula with the National EMS Education Standards (NEMSES), and four levels of licensure and certification were created.

5. **These individuals possess all EMT skills, as well as intravenous and intraosseous access, advanced airway devices, blood glucose monitoring, and administration of additional medications:**

A. Emergency Medical Responder (EMRs)
B. Emergency Medical Technicians (EMTs)
C. Advanced Emerency Medical Technicians (AEMTs)
D. Paramedics

Answer: C. Advanced Emergency Medical Technicians (AEMTs)

Explanation: Emergency Medical Responder (EMRs) provide basic and immediate care to patients who have issues with bleeding, require CPR or AED, and for women who having emergency childbirth. Emergency Medical Technician (EMTs) are all EMR providers who have additional skills in ventilation and oxygenation, pulse oximetry, vital sign monitoring, and administration of certain medications. Advanced Emergency Medical Technicians (AEMTs) possess all EMT skills, as well as intravenous and intraosseous access, advanced airway devices, blood glucose monitoring, and administration of additional medications. Paramedic are people who have management skills and advanced assessment abilities. This includes extensive pharmacology interventions, invasive skills, and the highest level of pre-hospital care allowed under the National EMS Education Standards.

6. **For adequate communication with other emergency care providers and healthcare workers, the EMT-B should:**

A. Be proficient in spoken grammar.
B. Be proficient in written grammar.
C. Avoid the use of slang terms.
D. All of the above.

Answer: D. All of the above.

Explanation: Good communication skills include refraining from phrases that are considered slang or that are unfamiliar to patients and other healthcare workers. Speaking in a well-educated manner is crucial in order to portray a professional image of yourself and the facility where you work. It is a must that an EMT-B is proficient in both written and spoken grammar.

7. **What are the ethical guidelines for emergency workers called?**

A. The National Emergency Responder Standards
B. The EMT Code of Ethics
C. The Emergency Provider Code of Ethics
D. The Code for Emergency Ethics

Answer: B. The EMT Code of Ethics

Explanation: Ethics are principles of conduct that govern a person or group. The National Association of Emergency Medical Technicians (NAEMT) adopted the EMT Code of Ethics in 1978, and this allows professions in this filed to have standards of ethics to adhere.

8. **What outlines the actions the emergency provider should legally perform based on certification level?**

A. The Standards of Practice
B. The Ethics of Practice
C. The Scope of Practice
D. The Hospital Practice Protocol

Answer: C. The Scope of Practice

Explanation: The scope of practice for the EMT-B outlines the actions the provider should legally perform based on certification level. The scope of practice is associated with licensure or certification status, not the person's experience, skill level, or knowledge base. Each state can determine the scope of practice for the EMS provider, and the National EMS Education Standards (NEMSES) aligns this scope throughout the United States.

9. **What question does the reasonable person test ask?**

A. What is reasonable for the patient at this time?
B. What should the EMT-B do in this situation?
C. What would a reasonable person with the same training do in this same situation?
D. What would a paramedic do in this same situation?

Answer: C. What would a reasonable person with the same training do in this same situation?

Explanation: A care standard is the degree of care a person is responsible for with a certain level of training when compared to someone with the exact same training who is performing the exact same task or skill. Standard of care involves the "reasonable person test," which is a question asking: What would a reasonable person with the same training do in this same situation? These standards require the EMT-Basic to perform an indicated assessment and treatment within his or her scope of practice.

10. Which advanced directive is an order that is specific to resuscitation efforts?

A. Living will
B. Consent form
C. Informed consent
D. Do Not Resuscitate (DNR) order

Answer: Do Not Resuscitate (DNR) order

Explanation: The DNR order is specific to which resuscitation efforts are allowed, and it does not apply to treatment that occurs before cardiac arrest. Broader than a DNR, the living will addresses healthcare wishes before the patient has a cardiac arrest. This may include feeding tubes, ventilator use, advanced airways, and other measures.

11. Which type of consent occurs when the patient is informed, of legal age, and is conscious and mentally competent?

A. Implied consent
B. Expressed consent
C. Social consent
D. Legal consent

Answer: B. Expressed consent

Explanation: Implied consent is assumed from the unconscious patient who requires emergency intervention. Implied consent is based on the assumption that the patient needs the life-saving interventions. With expressed consent, the patient must be able to make rational decisions, be of legal age, and be informed of all steps of the procedures, as well as procedural risks. With expressed consent, the patient is conscious and mentally competent to render treatment.

12. If a person is mentally incompetent, who should the EMT-B consult regarding the consent to treat?

A. The patient
B. A parent
C. A doctor
D. Any of the above

Answer: B. A parent

Explanation: For children and adults who are mentally disabled, the EMT-B must obtain consent from a parent or legal guardian. When a life-threatening issue arises, the consent for emergency treatment is rendered based on implied consent.

13. Which of the following would be considered an emancipated patient?

A. A 14 year old who is engaged.
B. A 16 year old pregnant female.
C. A 21 year old married male.
D. A 15 year old boy who says he lives all alone.

Answer: B. A 16 year old pregnant female.

Explanation: With emancipation issues, a patient legally under age should be recognized as having the legal capacity to give consent. Emancipated persons have criteria based on set regulations that vary state to state. Emancipated minors are those who are pregnant or married, people who are already a parent, members of the armed forces, persons emancipated by the courts, and those who are financially independent.

14. **Certain areas of liability apply to emergency responders and EMT professionals. When the person physically touches another person without his or her consent, it is called:**

A. Assault
B. Battery
C. Civil limits
D. Civil liability

Answer: Criminal liability involves assault, which is when a person is found guilty of harming another person by inflicting physical harm. However, physical contact is not always necessary for assault to apply. Battery is when the person physically touches another person without his or her consent. Civil liability is where a person can sue another for a wrongful act that results in some form of damage. Some civil suits involve just one EMS provider, but others involve all providers, as well as the medical director and supervisor of the EMS unit.

15. **When the EMT has failed to assess and treat the patient by standard care measures, it is called:**

A. Duty to act
B. Damage
C. Causation
D. Breach of duty

Answer: D. Breach of duty

Explanation: With negligence, the EMS provider is accused of some form of unintentional harm that occurs to a patient. This involves: duty to act, where the EMT has the obligation to respond and provide care; breach of duty, where the EMT has failed to assess and treat the patient by standard care measures; damage, where the patient experiences some form of injury due recognized in the legal system as worthy of compensation; causation, which is called proximate cause, and is an injury to a patient that was directly related to the EMT-B's breach of duty; and abandonment, which involves abandoning care provision.

16. In order to refuse treatment form EMS once called to a scene or house, the patient should be:

A. Mentally competent
B. Of legal age
C. Aware of his or her circumstances
D. All of the above

Answer: D. All of the above

Explanation: Refusal for treatment often occurs on emergency call outs. The competent patient may refuse treatment regardless of his or her condition. The refusal can present liability for the EMT-B, especially regarding abandonment and negligence issues. If this occurs, make attempts to contact the supervisor or medical director. To refuse treatment, the patient should be aware of his or her circumstances, aware of person, place, and time, of legal age, and mentally competent.

17. The EMT-B is authorized to release confidential information by law without the patient's consent or permission in all of these situations EXCEPT:

A. The third-party billing form requires the information.
B. The EMT-B is subpoenaed.
C. Another healthcare provider will be continuing care.
D. The information is requested by a reporter.

Answer: D. The information requested by a reporter.

Explanation: Confidential information requires a written release to be signed before it is sent or released. The EMS providers cannot release on request unless legal guardianship has been established or the patient specifically requests for this process. Certain state laws require reporting incidents, such as abuse or rape, and releasing information does not require consent in these incidents.

18. The normal anatomical position is:

A. The surface where any two points are taken.
B. An imaginary line drawn vertically through the patient's middle region of the body.
C. The patient facing forward with the palms also facing forward.
D. The patient sitting forward with the palms resting on the knees.

Answer: C. The patient facing forward with the palms also facing forward.

Explanation: An anatomical plane is surface where any two points are taken. To find this, a straight line is drawn to join these two points, within that surface of plane. The midline is when an imaginary line is drawn vertically through the patient's mid-body region. The normal anatomical position is when a person is facing forward with palms facing forward.

19. If a patient is lying on the belly or the front side of the body, which position is this?

A. Superior
B. Inferior
C. Anterior
D. Posterior

Answer: C. Anterior

Explanation: Superior is toward the head, or toward the upper body region. Inferior is toward the lower part of the body. Anterior (ventral) is on the belly or front side of the body. Posterior (dorsal) is on the buttocks or back side of the body.

20. What is the purpose of the respiratory system?

A. To move oxygen through the body and remove carbon dioxide from the body.
B. To move carbon dioxide through the body and remove oxygen from the body.
C. To move blood through the bod and filter waste from the body.
D. None of the above

Answer: A. To move oxygen through the body and remove carbon dioxide from the body.

21. When a person has bluish discoloration of the skin and lips, this is considered to be:

A. Dyspnea
B. Cyanosis
C. Epistaxis
D. Hemoptysis

Answer: B. Cyanosis

Explanation: Cyanosis is bluish discoloration of the skin or lips. Dyspnea is shortness of breath. Epistaxis is a nosebleed. Hemoptysis is coughing up blood.

22. When performing a respiratory assessment, the EMT-B should assess all of the following EXCEPT:

A. Rhythm
B. Breath sounds
C. Chest expansion
D. Volume

Answer: D. Volume

Explanation: The respiratory assessment involves rhythm (regular or irregular), breath sounds (present and equal vs. diminished or absent), chest expansion (adequate and equal vs. unequal and inadequate), and effort of breathing (no use vs. use of accessory muscles).

23. Which of the following is NOT one of the structures of the upper airway?

A. Trachea
B. Nasopharynx
C. Larynx
D. Epiglottis

Answer: A. Trachea

Explanation: The upper airway consists of the nose and mouth, nasopharynx (upper part of the throat behind the nose), oropharynx (area of the throat behind the mouth), larynx (voice box), and epiglottis (valve that protects the trachea opening). The trachea (windpipe) is part of the lower airway.

24. What is the area where the trachea branches into the bronchi called?

A. Alveoli
B. Carina
C. Bronchiole
D. Pleura

Answer: B. Carina

Explanation: The carina is area where trachea branches into bronchi. The bronchi are the right and left primary branches of the trachea leading to lungs. The bronchioles are the small branches of bronchi. The alveoli are small airway structures that diffuse oxygen from the respiratory system. The pleura are the two smooth layers of lung tissue that allow frictionless movement across one another.

25. Swelling due to fluid collection in the tissue is called:

A. Angina
B. Edema
C. Aneurysm
D. Hemolysis

Answer: B. Edema

Explanation: Angina is chest pain described as spasmodic and choking. An aneurysm is a bulging artery. Hemolysis is red blood cell breakdown.

26. The blood contains which percentage of plasma?

A. 25%
B. 51%
C. 75%
D. 91%

Answer: D. 91%

Explanation: The liquid part of the blood is called plasma, which is extracellular with 91% water. The cellular part of the blood contains leukocytes (white blood cells WBCs), erythrocytes (red blood cells or RBCs), and thrombocytes (platelets).

27. Which vessels of the circulatory system transport blood away from the heart?

A. Veins
B. Capillaries
C. Venules
D. Arteries

Answer: D. Arteries

Explanation: Arteries lead away from the heart and branch into arterioles. Veins lead to the heart and branch into venules. Capillaries connect between arterioles and venules, which are small venous structures that deliver blood.

28. The heart layer that is thick and muscular and considered the heart wall is the:

A. Endocardium
B. Myocardium
C. Epicardium
D. Pericardium

Answer: B. Myocardium

Explanation: Endocardium is the smooth lining inside the heart. Myocardium is the thick muscular heart wall. Epicardium is the outer layer of the heart and inner layer of pericardium. Pericardium is the fibrous sac around the heart.

29. The lower heart chambers that receive blood from the atria and send it throughout the body during ventricular contraction are the:

A. Atria
B. Ventricles
C. Valves
D. Systems

Answer: B. Ventricles

Explanation: The atria are the two upper heart chambers. The atria pump blood into the ventricles right before they contract, which is called an "atrial kick." The ventricles are the lower heart chambers that receive blood from the atria and send it throughout the body during ventricular contraction. Ventricular contraction generates a palpable pulse. The heart valves are one-way valves that are between the atria and ventricles, which allow blood to move in a downward direction into the ventricles during atrial contraction.

30. What is the primary pacemaker of the heart called?

A. The atrioventricular (AV) junction
B. The sinoatrial (SA) node
C. The atriosinal (AS) junction
D. The sinoventricular (SV) node

Answer: B. The sinoatrial (SA) node

Explanation: The heart has a conduction (electrical) system, which generates electrical impulses and stimulates heart muscle contraction. The primary area is the sinoatrial (SA) node, which generates anywhere from 60 to 100 impulses per minute in the adult. The backup pacemaker is the atrioventricular (AV) junction, which generates electrical impulses at around 40 to 60 per minute. The Bundle of His is a pacemaker that can generate around 20 to 40 impulses per minute.

31. The ability of the heart to contract, which requires adequate blood volume and muscle strength is called:

A. Preload
B. Afterload
C. Myocardial contractility
D. Ventricular contractility

Answer: C. Myocardial contractility

Explanation: Myocardial contractility is the ability of the heart to contract, which requires adequate blood volume and muscle strength. Preload is the pre-contraction pressure that is based on the amount of blood that flows back to the heart. An increased preload leads to increased ventricular stretching of the ventricles and increased contractility. Afterload is the resistance which the heart must overcome during contraction of the ventricles. If there is an increase in afterload, there is decreased cardiac output.

32. What is compromised when inadequate blood perfusion occurs?

A. Blood volume
B. Blood cells
C. Blood flow
D. Blood clots

Answer: C. Blood flow

Explanation: Blood perfusion is the flow of blood through the body. When there is adequate perfusion, the organs and tissues receive oxygen-rich blood. However, with inadequate perfusion, also called shock, the blood flow is compromised.

33. All of the following are functions of the musculoskeletal system EXCEPT:

A. It connects structures.
B. It protects organs.
C. It assists with movement
D. It forms body shape.

Answer: A. It connects structures.

Explanation: The musculoskeletal system is comprised of the bony skeleton, skeletal muscles, cardiac muscles, and smooth muscles. There also are 206 bones, as well as cartilage and ligaments. The muscular system protects the organs, produces heat, assists with movement, and forms body shape.

34. The femur, tibia, fibula, humerus, ulna, and radius are all considered to be:

A. Flat bones
B. Irregular bones
C. Sesamoid bones
D. Long bones

Answer: D. Long bones

Explanation: Long bones are tubular, such as the femur, tibia, and radius.

35. Which bone is a Sesamoid bone?

A. Carpal
B. Zygoma
C. Patella
D. Scapula

Answer: C. Patella

Explanation: Sesamoid bones are round, such as the patella. Short bones, also called cuboidal bones, include the carpals and tarsals. Flat bones include the sternum, skull, and scapula. Irregular bones are of varied shapes, such as the vertebrae and zygoma.

36. The axial skeleton is made up of all of the following EXCEPT:

A. Facial bones

B. Hyoid bone

C. Spine

D. Carpals

Answer: D. Carpals

Explanation: The axial skeleton contains the skull, spinal column, and rib cage. Small bones included are the facial bones, hyoid bone, and the vertebra of the spine.

37. The EMT-B is on the scene of a car accident. One patient cannot open his mouth and complains of jaw pain. What movable portion of the jaw is likely injured?

A. The occipital bone

B. The temporal bone

C. The mandible bone

D. The zygomatic bone

Answer: C. The mandible bone

Explanation: The skull bones include the frontal (forehead bone), parietal (bone on top of the head), occipital (bone in the back of the skull), temporal (lateral bones above the cheekbones), maxillae (bones that form the upper jaw), mandible (the moveable portion of the lower jaw), zygomatic (the cheekbones), nasal (the bone of the nose), and foramen magnum (the opening in the occipital bone to connect brain with spinal cord).

38. A patient has an injury to the pelvis. The EMT-B understands that which of the following bones could be fractured?

A. Ilium

B. Ischium

C. Pubis

D. Any or all of the above

Answer: The pelvic bones include the ilium (upper area of the pelvis), the ischium (lower area of the pelvis), and the pubis (anterior portion of the pelvis).

39. The shoulder joint is considered which type of joint?

A. Symphysis joint
B. Hinge joint
C. Ball-and-socket joint
D. Latissimus joint

Answer: C. Ball-and-socket joint

Explanation: A symphysis joint has limited movement, such as the symphysis pubis. A hinge joint is where bones can only move in one direction, as with the knee. The shoulder is a ball-and-socket joint, where the distal ends of the bones have free motion.

40. You are caring for a trauma patient who has suffered a brain injury. She cannot breathe on her own, so which area do you suspect is injured?

A. Cerebellum
B. Cerebrum
C. Brain stem
D. Dura mater

Answer: C. Brain stem

Explanation: The cerebrum controls memory, thought, and senses. The cerebellum coordinates movement, balance, and fine motor ability. The brain stem controls breathing and consciousness.

41. How many pairs of cranial nerves are in the human body?

A. 6
B. 12
C. 24
D. 28

Answer: B. 12

Explanation: The human body has 12 pair of cranial nerves and 31 pair of spinal nerves.

42. Which portion of the autonomic nervous system regulates the "fight or flight" response?

A. Sympathetic system
B. Peripheral nervous system
C. Parasympathetic system
D. Cranial system

Answer: A. Sympathetic system

Explanation: The autonomic nervous system (ANS) is the involuntary portion of the PNS. The two portions of this system are: sympathetic - "Fight or flight" which works in times of stress and parasympathetic - "Feed and breed" which controls rest, reproduction, and digestion.

43. Of total body weight, what percentage of it is skin weight?

A. 6%
B. 10%
C. 14%
D. 18%

Answer: D. 18%

Explanation: The integument is the skin, which makes up around 18% of the body's weight. Skin is necessary to protect a person from the invasion of microorganisms, as well as to regulate body temperature and manufacture vitamins. The skin and accessory structures (glands, nails, and hair) make up the integumentary system. The three layers of the skin are the epidermis, the dermis, and the subcutaneous tissue (hypodermis).

44. The digestive organ that lies in the left upper quadrant and receives and breaks down food is the:

A. Esophagus
B. Stomach
C. Small intestines
D. Pancreas

Answer: B. Stomach

Explanation: The abdominal cavity is separated from the thoracic cavity by the diaphragm. The esophagus is the tube that runs from the mouth to the stomach and lies behind the trachea. The stomach is the digestive organ that lies in the LUQ and receives and breaks down food. The pancreas is an organ of the RUQ that aids in digestion, produces insulin, and regulates blood sugar. The small intestine is a hollow tubular organ in both lower quadrants that digests fat and releases enzymes. The large intestine is a hollow organ of the lower abdomen that pulls out liquid and forms solid stool.

45. The operational units of the kidneys are known as the:

A. Cortexes
B. Hilum
C. Ureters
D. Nephrons

Answer: D. Nephrons

Explanation: The urinary system controls fluid balance and filters waste from the blood via the kidneys. The ureters are two tubes that connect each kidney to the bladder. Urine moves from the kidneys, through the ureters, and then down the urethra to exit the body. This system works with the reproductive system to remove metabolic waste materials from the body, such as uric acid, urea, nitrogenous waste, and creatinine. The urinary system also maintains electrolyte balance and assists the liver in body detoxification. The hilum is the middle section of the kidney, and the nephrons are the operational units.

46. Regarding the male reproductive system structures, what sac encloses the testes?

A. Seminal
B. Bulbourethral
C. Vas deferens
D. Scrotal

Answer: D. Scrotal

Explanation: The scrotum, or scrotal sac, encloses the testes. The testes (gonads) are structures that produce sperm and testosterone. The vas deferens are tubular structures at the end of the epididymis. The bulbourethral bland is the gland that secretes a tiny amount of seminal fluid. The seminal ducts are structures that transport sperm from the testes to the exterior. The seminal vesicles are structures that produce most seminal fluid.

47. What structures of the female reproductive system produce ova (eggs) and hormones?

A. Fallopian tubes
B. Ovaries
C. Uterus
D. Ureters

Answer: B. Ovaries

Explanation: The female organs are the ovaries, fallopian tubes, and the vagina. The female reproductive system protects the fertilized ovum (egg) for the nine-month gestation period. The external structures enhance sexual stimulation and protect the body from foreign materials. The ovaries are internal structures that produce and release the ovum.

48. When moving a patient who is injured with the power lift, the EMT-B should:

A. Keep the person close to his or her body
B. Use the legs when lifting.
C. Use a power grip.
D. All of the above.

Answer: D. All of the above.

Explanation: When using power lift, keep the person or object close to his or her body, use the legs (not the back) for lifting, use a power grip, where the palms are up and all fingers are firmly grasped around the object, be sure to get enough help for the job, and prepare the lift before the process to reduce distance the self and avoid problems.

49. After placing a patient on a blanket, the EMS providers decide to move him away from the accident scene, due to a small car fire. What emergency move should they consider?

A. The armpit-forearm drag
B. The shirt drag
C. The blanket drag
D. The power lift

Answer: C. The blanket drag

Explanation: Emergency moves are used when the scene appears to be dangerous. The patient should be moved before giving any type of care. Emergency moves include: the shirt drag, which is pulling on the patient's clothing at the shoulder or neck area; the blanket drag, which is dragging or pulling the patient on a blanket; and the armpit-forearm drag, which is putting hands under the patient's armpits from the back, and grasping the forearms while dragging the patient.

50. What is the minimum number of providers needed for the direct ground lift?

A. 1
B. 2
C. 3
D. 4

Answer: C. 3

Explanation: With this lift, only use when there is no suspected spine injury. Two or three rescuers must line up on one side of the patient, and one EMS provider places the patient's arms on his or her chest. Therefore, at least three are needed. The rescuer at the head places one arm under the patient's neck and shoulder, and then places the other under the patient's lower back, the second rescuer places one arm under the patient's knees and one arm above the buttocks, and the third rescuer places both arms under the waist and the other two slide arms either up to the mid-back or down to the buttocks. After the signal, all three rescuers lift the patient to their knees and roll the patient toward his or her chest. On signal, the rescuers rise and position the patient on the stretcher.

51. Which type of equipment is used mainly for cervical spine immobilization, and allows for CPR? It is lightweight and requires a four-person lift.

A. Scoop stretcher
B. Backboard
C. Half board
D. Cervical collar

Answer: B. Backboard

Explanation: The scoop stretcher is a unit that divides into two long pieces, either left and right or top and bottom. This stretcher allows for easy positioning with very little patient movement, and is good to reduce patient discomfort during transfer. The backboard is a device used mainly for cervical spine immobilization, and allows for CPR. It is lightweight and requires a four-person lift.

52. You are transferring a patient to the hospital after leaving an accident scene. He is intoxicated and combative. The team has applied soft restraints. What should the EMT-B monitor?

A. LOC
B. Vital signs
C. Distal circulation
D. All of the above

Answer: D. All of the above

Explanation: Monitor the patient's vital signs, level of consciousness, airway, and distal circulation (below the restraints). Document the reason for the use of mechanical restraints, as well as the duration, method, and assessment process. Never restrain a patient in the prone position or leave the patient unsupervised.

53. A requirement for oxygen occurs during activity, injury, and illness, with the primary methods controlling oxygen delivery being:

A. Increased breathing rate
B. Decreased breathing rate
C. Increased or decreased tidal volume of breaths
D. All of the above

Answer: D. All of the above

Explanation: Exhalation is a passive part of ventilation and requires no energy. With exhalation, the intercostal muscles and diaphragm relaxes, the thorax decreases and air leaves the lungs. As exhalation occurs, intra-thoracic pressure will exceed atmospheric pressure. A requirement for oxygen occurs during activity, injury, and illness, with the primary methods controlling oxygen delivery being increased or decreased breathing rate, as well as increased or decreased tidal volume of breaths.

54. What is the normal respiratory rate for an adult?

A. 10 to 15 breaths per minute
B. 12 to 20 breaths per minute
C. 15 to 30 breaths per minute
D. 25 to 50 breaths per minute

Explanation: Adults: 12 to 20 breaths per minute, children: 15 to 30 breaths per minute, and infants: 25 to 50 breaths per minute.

55. What is the main cause of airway obstruction?

A. Foreign object
B. Swelling of the throat
C. Tongue
D. Fluid

Answer: C. Tongue

Explanation: With airway obstruction, there is blockage of an airway structure that leads to the alveoli. This leads to lack of effective ventilation. The causes of an airway obstruction include tongue (main cause of airway obstruction), swelling of the throat, foreign bodies (toys, food, or an object), and fluid (blood, saliva, vomit, and mucus).

56. Once an airway is established, it may become blocked with saliva, blood, vomit, mucus, broken teeth, or food. Should this occur, the EMT-B must clear the airway so the material does not go into the lungs. The best technique to clear the airway is:

A. Manual removal with fingers.
B. Roll the patient to his or her side to allow fluids to drain.
C. Suction with a device.
D. Use a gauze pad to soak up fluid

Answer: B. Roll the patient to his or her side to allow fluids to drain.

Explanation: Once an airway is established, it may become blocked. Should this occur, the EMT-B must clear the airway so the material does not go into the lungs. The best technique to clear the airway is to roll the patient on his or her side to allow fluids to drain from the mouth.

57. One form of oxygenation that should not be used on young children or infants is:

A. Mouth-to-mouth
B. Mouth-to-mask
C. Bag-valve mask (BVM)
D. Flow-restricted, oxygen-powered ventilation

Answer: D. Flow-restricted, oxygen-powered ventilation

Explanation: The flow-restricted, oxygen-powered ventilation device works similarly to the BVM. After the airway is cleared, a flow-restricted device is attached to the mask, and there is no bag. This device cannot be used on young children and infants, due to the risk of lung damage. Steps for use include: keep 4th and 5th digits of your hand under the patient's jaw to lift the chin, depress the button to trigger the device to administer oxygen, as the patient's chest rises, stop the device so the patient can exhale, and repeat this once every five seconds.

58. Which device delivers a low concentration of oxygen to the patient?

A. Nasal cannula
B. Nonrebreather mask
C. Flow-restricted, oxygen-powered ventilation
D. Bag-valve mask (BVM)

Answer: A. Nasal cannula

Explanation: The nasal cannula delivers a low concentration of oxygen to the patient. The small piece of tubing attaches to the patient's nose, and oxygen flows directly into the nostrils. The nonrebreather mask delivers a high oxygen concentration, and comes in many sizes that can be attached to a bag that stores oxygen. The mask is placed over the patient's mouth and nose, and the patient must breathe in the oxygen from the bag.

59. What is the first component of the patient assessment, once the EMS unit arrives on the accident, injury, or illness scene?

A. Primary assessment
B. Patient history
C. Scene size up
D. Scene observation

Answer: C. Scene size up

Explanation: The five components of patient assessment include scene size up, primary assessment, patient history, secondary assessment, and reassessment. The priority of each component is based on the patient's chief complaint (CC) and current condition. Trauma patients demand more primary and secondary assessment than other conscious persons. Regardless of the patient's current status, the patient assessment has to be organized and methodical.

60. When assessing a patient, you notice a heart rate of 48 beats per minute. The patient is alert, oriented, talking, and has no obvious bleeding or trauma. What medication could cause this?

A. Nitroglycerine
B. Digoxin
C. Insulin
D. Aspirin

Answer: B. Digoxin

Explanation: The heart beats a certain number of times each minute. This is considered the heart or pulse rate. The normal adult pulse rate at rest is from 60 to 100 beats per minute. A rapid heart rate occurs from infection, dehydration, shock, anemia, stress, anxiety, thyroid conditions, and heart conditions. A slow pulse rate can occur from certain medications (beta blockers and digoxin), a vasovagal response, and various cardiac conditions.

61. Elevated body temperature (fever) is often a symptom of:

    A. Infection
    B. Stress
    C. Dehydration
    D. All of the above

Answer: D. All of the above

Explanation: Elevated temperature (fever) is often a symptom of infection or inflammation, but some elderly people do not exhibit a high body temperature with illness. Conditions that often raise body temperature include infection, stress, dehydration, exercise, the environment, and thyroid disorders. When someone gets cold from weather, exposure to the elements, or experiences shock or a thyroid disorder, a drop in body temperature occurs. Any temperature of 95 F degrees or lower is defined as hypothermia.

62. Written as two numbers, a healthy blood pressure is a systolic value of ___ to ___ and a diastolic value of ___ to ___.

    A. 90 to 150 and 40 to 70
    B. 95 to 145 and 45 to 75
    C. 100 to 139 and 60 to 79
    D. 89 to 129 and 50 to 89

Answer: C. 100 to 139 and 60 to 79

Explanation: Blood pressure has two numbers, the top is the systolic pressure, and the bottom number is a diastolic pressure. The systolic pressure is the first distinct sound of the blood flowing through the artery with the use of a blood pressure cuff. Written as two numbers, a healthy blood pressure is a systolic value of 100 to 139 and a diastolic value of 60 to 79.

63. All of the following are common causes of hypotension EXCEPT:

A. Hypothermia
B. Indigestion
C. Shock
D. Syncope

Answer: B. Indigestion

Explanation: Hypotension (low BP) can be caused by hypothermia, shock, and syncope. Also, older people often experience orthostatic hypotension, which occurs when standing up too quickly. Other factors that cause hypotension include arrhythmias like atrial fibrillation and bradycardia, diuretics, and digitalis.

64. Hidden injuries can occur as the result of all of the following EXCEPT:

A. Seat belts
B. Air bags
C. Steering wheel
D. Floor mats

Answer: D. Floor mats

Explanation: A seat belt does not guarantee the patient did not receive injury. Also, the air bags can lead to injury, and may not be effective without seat belt use. The patient can hit the steering wheel after deflation, and if left deployed, the air bag can cause deformities.

65. You are assessing the patient using the OPQRST method. In this mnemonic, what does the "P" stand for?

A. Provocation
B. Pulse
C. Pressure
D. Pain

Answer: A. Provocation

Explanation: Provocation means what caused the symptoms or made them worse. The O is for onset, the Q is for quality, the R is for radiation, the S is for severity, and the T is for time.

66. Patients are considered high-risk if they possess certain injuries or have existing medical conditions. For adults, these include:

A. A bleeding disorder
B. On anticoagulant therapy
C. Immunocompromised
D. All of the above

Answer: D. All of the above

Explanation: High-risk patients are those older than 55 years, people with respiratory or cardiovascular disease, those with a bleeding disorder or who are on anticoagulants, and the immunocompromised patient.

67. Regarding protecting yourself against harmful substances, infections, and injury, what does BSI mean?

A. Body substance isolation
B. Body security instructions
C. Best substance isolation
D. Best safety instructions

Answer: A. Body substance isolation

Explanation: The EMT-B must take necessary body substance isolation (BSI) precautions. BSI includes wearing appropriate protective gear, such as gloves, gowns, masks, and goggles. Always keep a spare pair of gloves in case contamination occurs. These precautions protect the EMS providers, victims, and bystanders. Personal protective equipment (PPE) is needed when there are potentially dangerous situations, such as rescue missions, hazardous materials emergencies, and violent scenes.

68. Any incident that led to the patient's trauma, wounds, or affliction is considered:

A. The scene size up
B. The mechanism of injury (MOI)
C. The chief complaint (CC)
D. The manner of accident (MOA)

Answer: B. The mechanism of injury (MOI)

Explanation: The mechanism of injury (MOI) is any incident that led to the patient's trauma, wounds, or affliction. Sometimes, this is determined prior to EMS arrival on the scene. The MOI may be uncertain in some situations, so you should attempt to determine what happened exactly. Some instances, the MOI is spotted immediately, such as an icy road or a step of stairs. Also, if the victim is unconscious, ask any bystanders or witnesses.

69. Of the following, which is NOT one of the four categories of mental status assessment?

A. Alert
B. Verbal
C. Painful
D. Unstable

Answer: D. Unstable

Explanation: The patient's mental status should be assessed immediately when the EMS providers arrive. The four categories of mental status assessment are AVPU: Alert - Does the patient respond to basic questions or the presence of the service provider? Verbal - The patient responds to the EMT-B's voice, but is unaware of the person's presence. Sometimes, when the EMT-B raises his or her voice, a change in tone will provoke a response. Painful - Does the patient respond to painful stimuli? This is often found when the provider elicits a response. Unresponsive - Does the patient respond to verbal or painful stimuli? If the patient is unresponsive, he or she should be considered for priority transport.

70. What patient would warrant a rapid head-to-toe trauma assessment to look for hidden or internal injuries?

A. Vehicle rollover
B. Penetration to the chest
C. Serious fall
D. Two vehicle crash

Answer: D. Two vehicle crash

Explanation: Trauma patients often have a high-risk MOI, or even an unknown MOI. Do a rapid head-to-toe trauma assessment to find possible hidden or internal injuries. These occur from things like ejection from a moving vehicle, a serious fall, a vehicle rollover, or penetration to the head/chest/abdomen.

71. The EMS provider should do ongoing assessment once every __ minutes for the stable patient, and every __ minutes for an unstable patient.

A. 10 and 3
B. 12 and 5
C. 15 and 5
D. 30 and 15

Answer: C. 15 and 5

Explanation: The EMS provider should do ongoing assessment once every 15 minutes for the stable patient, and every 5 minutes for an unstable patient.

72. All of the following are part of an ongoing assessment EXCEPT:

A. Evaluation of mental status
B. Assess skin color, condition, temperature, and perfusion.
C. Assess airway, breathing, and pulse
D. Document patient's explanation of the event.

Answer: D. Document patient's explanation of the event.

Explanation: An ongoing assessment involves repeat initial assessment, determine mental status, assess airway, breathing, and pulse, assess skin color, condition, temperature, and perfusion, identify priority patients, record vital signs, repeat focuses assessment, and check intervention.

73. For elderly and geriatric patients, which of the following would NOT affect the patient's respiratory status?

A. Impaired gas exchange
B. Risk of infection
C. Loss of muscle coordination
D. Loss of skin elasticity

Answer: D. Loss of skin elasticity

Explanation: With older people, alveolar surfaces degenerate, so gas exchange is impaired, the pulmonary musculature is diminished in size and strength, lung elasticity is often lost with age as the ribs get less pliable, the pulmonary system is more at risk for infection and disease, and there is less gas exchange and loss of muscle coordination.

74. When assessing an elderly man, you notice that he doesn't hear well and he cannot see well. It is dark and you are moving him into the ambulance for transport. What should the EMT-B suspect to be the cause?

A. An infection
B. A serious injury
C. Advancing age
D. All of the above

Answer: C. Advancing age

Explanation: Older people have many neurological system changes. These include loss of neurons and decreased mass of brain, reflexes are slowed due to nerve cell degeneration, decreased night vision and loss of hearing, and deterioration of nervous system leads to high incidence of falls and inability to adapt to stressors.

75. **You are responding to a call where a 78-year-old man is confused and has developed incontinence. He is on many medications, so you suspect drug toxicity. Why would this occur?**

A. Loss of nephrons results in decreased kidney size.
B. Electrolytes are affected by medications.
C. Renal changes result in decreased waste filtration and the possibility of drug toxicity.
D. Reduced renal blood flow leads to vascular dilation.

Answer: C. Renal changes result in decreased waste filtration and the possibility of drug toxicity.

Explanation: For the elderly person, there is a loss of nephrons results in decreased kidney size and function, electrolytes are often disturbed, which affect kidney filtration, and reduced renal blood flow occurs due to vascular stenosis. All changes result in decreased waste filtration, electrolyte disturbances, and the possibility of drug toxicity.

76. **When should the EMT-B contact radio dispatch?**

A. When you receive the initial call.
B. When you arrive on the scene.
C. When you leave for the hospital.
D. All of the above.

Answer: D. All of the above.

Explanation: When the EMT-B uses the radio dispatch, be sure to state the unit's location, that you received and understand the call, and that you are responding at present. Contact the dispatcher once you reach the patient(s) and scene. Be sure to record the arrival time, when you leave the scene with the patient, when you arrive to the trauma center or hospital, and when you arrive back to your station.

77. On the minimum data set, what should EMS providers obtain?

A. Patient information
B. Administrative information
C. Both A and B
D. Neither A nor B

Answer: C. Both A and B

Explanation: EMS providers are required to obtain two sets of information when going out on a patient call: patient information and administrative information, as on the minimum data sets.

78. The pre-hospital care report is only used by:

A. EMS providers
B. Insurance companies
C. Healthcare providers
D. All of the above

Answer: D. All of the above

Explanation: The pre-hospital report is a legal document, is considered confidential, and should be not read or shared with other people. This report gives information regarding the patient's status when the EMTs arrived on the scene and as they transferred the patient. This documentation is read by doctors, surgeons, nurses, and insurance companies to determine the type of care required for that person. The pre-hospital care report is only used by qualified medical personnel and anyone who is involved with the patient's ongoing care.

79. Who should the EMT-B contact if he or she has a question regarding patient competence concerning patient refusal?

A. The medical director
B. The supervisor
C. Either A or B
D. Neither A nor B

Answer: C. Either A or B

Explanation: If the patient is alert, competent, and not under the influence of alcohol or drugs, he or she has the right to refuse treatment by EMS if they are called. If the provider has a concern or question regarding a patient's competence, he or she should contact the supervisor or medical director before leaving the scene. Offer the patient various alternatives to transportation to the hospital, and if the patient continues to refuse, have the medical director or the patient's primary physician speak with him or her. Before leaving the scene, the EMT-B must have the patient sign a refusal form.

80. Which route of medication administration is used for mists, sprays, and mask delivered drugs?

A. Buccal
B. Inhalation
C. Intradermal
D. Subcutaneous

Answer: B. Inhalation

Explanation: The buccal route is where the medication is placed between the cheek and gum via spray, gel, or tablet. Examples: nitroglycerine and glucose. With inhalation medications are inhaled into the respiratory system via mists, sprays, and masks. Examples: oxygen and albuterol. The intradermal (ID) route involves medicine being injected into the dermal skin layer at a 15 degree angle via a 25 - 27 gauge needle. Subcutaneous (SC) medications are injected into the subcutaneous tissue at a 45 - 90 degree angle via a 22 to 25 gauge needle, as with insulin.

81. All of the following side effects are possible with glucose administration EXCEPT:

A. Dizziness
B. Confusion
C. Hyperglycemia
D. Nausea

Answer: D. Nausea

Explanation: Side effects to glucose include dizziness, confusion, and elevation of glucose in the blood stream, which could lead to hyperglycemia.

82. What is activated oral charcoal used to treat?

A. Poisoning when emesis is contraindicated.
B. Poisoning when emesis is not contraindicated.
C. Renal toxicity.
D. Dehydration.

Answer: A. Poisoning when emesis is contraindicated.

Explanation: Charcoal is an adsorbent and it works to adsorb various toxins through chemical binding and prevents GI adsorption. It is indicated for poisoning when emesis is contraindicated. Given PO, the dosage is 1 g/kg (50 to 75 kg) mixed with water.

83. Of the following, which medications would interact with epinephrine?

A. Digoxin
B. Monoamine oxidase inhibitors
C. Beta blockers
D. Aspirin

Answer: B. Monoamine oxidase inhibitors

Explanation: Epinephrine is a sympathetic drug used for broncho-constrictions, hypotension from anaphylaxis, and acute allergic reaction. Drug interactions include monoamine oxidase (MAO) inhibitors and bretylium, which potentiate epinephrine.

84. How does albuterol sulfate work?

A. It relaxes the cardiac muscle and allows better oxygen-rich blood flow.
B. It relaxes the smooth muscle of the alveoli and the distal vasculature.
C. It relaxes the smooth muscle of the bronchial tree and the peripheral vasculature.
D. All of the above.

Answer: C. It relaxes the smooth muscle of the bronchial tree and the peripheral vasculature.

Explanation: Albuterol is a selective beta-2 adrenergic bronchodilator. It relaxes smooth muscle of the bronchial tree and the peripheral vasculature, and starts to work within 5 to 15 minutes. It is indicated for the relief of bronchospasms.

85. Of the following, which is NOT an effect of atropine?

A. Pupil dilation
B. Decreased heart rate
C. Inhibits GI secretions
D. Decreases GI motility

Answer: B. Decreased heart rate

Explanation: Atropine is an antimuscarinic, anticholinergic, and parasympathetic blocker. Its mechanism of action involves blocking acetylcholine (ACh) at the muscarinic receptor sites. The effects of atropine are the opposite of parasympathetic nervous system stimulation, as it blocks the action of the ACh. It increases heart rate, force of contraction, and conduction, inhibits glandular section in the respiratory tract and relaxes the bronchial tree muscle for broncho-dilation, inhibits GI secretions and decreases GI motility, dilates the pupils, and decreases normal bladder tone and intensity.

86. Which of the following patients would be treated by an EMT-B with pralidoxime (2-PAM)?

A. A 32-year-old man poisoned by a pesticide.
B. A 24-year-old woman poisoned by alcohol.
C. A 55-year-old woman who has ingested marijuana.
D. A 66-year-old man with an elevated heart rate.

Answer: A. A 32-year-old man poisoned by a pesticide.

Explanation: Pralidoxime (2-PAM) is the antidote to cholinesterase inhibitors and organophosphate pesticides and chemicals. When used with atropine, it treats poisoning caused by pesticides and nerve gases. Side effects include double vision, rapid breathing, dizziness, palpitations, and muscle stiffness or weakness.

87. Which of the following patients should NOT receive aspirin if chest pain were to occur, unless the medical director advises you to administer this?

A. A 29-year-old man who uses cocaine.
B. A 70-year-old woman with a history of GI bleeding.
C. A 65-year-old man who has taken an aspirin earlier.
D. A 45-year-old woman who eats broccoli.

Answer: B. A 70-year-old woman with a history of GI bleeding.

Explanation: Aspirin is a platelet inhibitor and anti-inflammatory agent, and it works by blocking platelet aggregation. It is contraindicated in people with known hypersensitivity or allergy. Aspirin should be used with caution for patients with GI bleeding and GI upset.

88. A chronic respiratory condition that many EMS providers must treat from time to time, which is characterized by airway inflammation that has two phases of responses is:

A. Asthma
B. COPD
C. Influenza
D. Bronchitis

Answer: A. Asthma

Explanation: Asthma is a chronic respiratory condition that many EMS providers must treat from time to time. This common illness is characterized by airway inflammation that has two phases of responses. During the first phase, fluid leads from the capillaries and that leads to bronchial constriction and reduced expiratory air flow. With the second phase, the swelling cases further difficulties with expiratory flow of air, and this often occurs around 6 to 8 hours after the onset of the asthma attack.

89. A "blue bloater" is a patient who has:

A. Asthma
B. Emphysema
C. Chronic bronchitis
D. Acute bronchitis

Answer: C. Chronic bronchitis

Explanation: Many patients with a chronic form of COPD, called emphysema, have a prolonged expiratory phase and increased red blood cell production, which gives the skin a pinkish tone (pink puffers). Chronic bronchitis results from excessive mucus production in the respiratory tract. The alveoli often become obstructed by mucus clogs, and the patient can become cyanotic and swollen (blue bloaters). The EMS provider will often have to administer oxygen to COPD patients who are in distress.

90. Upper airway obstruction can occur from all of the following EXCEPT:

A. Burns
B. Allergic reactions
C. Trauma
D. Mucus buildup

Answer: D. Mucus buildup

Explanation: Upper airway obstruction occurs from blockage of the trachea, voice box, and throat. Many causes of this include allergic reactions, burns, infections, trauma, aspiration of foreign bodies, or blockage from the tongue. Lower airway obstruction is when there is blockage of the lower trachea or lungs. This often occurs from mucus or fluid buildup or directly from inflammation.

91. When a patient is in respiratory distress, he or she often will have:

A. Decreased respiratory rate
B. Depletion of carbon dioxide
C. Excessive utilization of oxygen
D. None of the above

Answer: D. None of the above

Explanation: Respiratory distress occurs when respiratory distress causes the body to require more oxygen. The main symptom of respiratory distress is difficulty breathing, but other symptoms can be increased respiratory rate, altered rhythm of breathing, and reduced quality or depth of breathing. This can result in retention of carbon dioxide and inability to utilize oxygen.

92. To assess a patient with a respiratory disorder, the EMT-B should look for:

A. Hypoinflation of the chest
B. Hyperinflation of the chest
C. Both A and B
D. Neither A nor B

Answer: B. Hyperinflation of the chest

Explanation: For the patient with a respiratory disorder, the EMT-B should assess presenting signs and symptoms, and look for hyperinflation of the chest.

93. Of the following, which condition would be considered if a child 2 years old has a seal-type bark and dyspnea?

A. Common cold
B. Pneumonia
C. Croup
D. Asthma

Answer: C. Croup

Explanation: The common cold is a viral illness that can lead to mild dyspnea, but no seal bark. Pneumonia can be viral or bacterial, and is an infection that leads to fluid accumulation in the interstitial space between the alveolus and capillary. It also can cause coughing and dyspnea. Croup is more common among young children 3 years and younger, and it involves an inflammation of the lining of the larynx. Croup is characterized by a "seal bark" and dyspnea.

94. Of the following signs and symptoms, which is NOT typically seen with shock (hypoperfusion)?

A. Weak pulse
B. Rapid breathing
C. Cyanosis
D. Warm, flushed skin

Answer: D. Warm, flushed skin

Explanation: Shock (hypoperfusion) is a profound depression of the body's vital processes. It is characterized by signs and symptoms of paleness, cyanosis, cool clammy skin, shallow and rapid breathing, rapid but weak pulse, mental dullness, restlessness, and anxiety. Also, there is a reduction in blood volume, so low or decreasing blood pressure is seen, as is subnormal body temperature.

95. When cardiac compromise occurs, the patient may complain of all of the following EXCEPT:

A. Feeling of impending doom
B. Diaphoresis and sweating
C. A squeezing chest pain
D. A dry cough

Answer: D. A dry cough

Explanation: Symptoms and signs of cardiac compromise include a feeling of impending doom, squeezing, chest pain or dull pressure that may radiate down the arm or to the jaw, sudden onset of diaphoresis (sweating), anxiety and irritability, difficulty breathing, irregular or abnormal pulse rate, abnormal blood pressure, epigastric pain, and nausea and/or vomiting.

96. Angina is transient chest pain that results from:

A. Too much carbon dioxide.
B. Lack of oxygen to the heart muscle.
C. Lack of blood flow to the lungs.
D. Too much fluid in the left ventricle.

Answer: B. Lack of oxygen to the heart muscle.

Explanation: Angina is transient chest pain that results from a lack of oxygen to the heart muscle. This can occur at rest or during physical activity or stress. It resolves with rest, oxygen, and nitroglycerine. Angina only last around 5 to 15 minutes, and does not cause permanent heart damage.

97. The EMS provider should treat the patient with chest pain as if he or she:

A. Is having angina.
B. Is having a myocardial infarction.
C. Is in congestive heart failure
D. All of the above.

Answer: B. Is having a myocardial infarction.

Explanation: With acute myocardial infarction (MI), there is actual death to a region of the cardiac muscle from lack of oxygenated blood flow, usually from blocked coronary arteries. The symptoms of angina and MI are similar, but MI pain atypically does not go away after a few minutes. The EMS provider should treat the patient with chest pain as if he or she is having an MI.

98. Of the three types of cardiac polarity, which one is the electrical status of the heart muscle cells when they attempt to maintain electronegativity inside the cells for distribution of ions (potassium, sodium, and chloride)?

A. Polarization
B. Depolarization
C. Repolarization
D. Inpolarization

Answer: A. Polarization

Explanation: Electrocardiography involves heart activity. The electrical activity of the heart follows a conductive pathway resulting in the cardiac cycle (heart pumping blood). There are three types of cardiac polarity: polarization, depolarization, and repolarization. Polarity is the electrical status of cardiac muscle cells in an attempt to maintain electronegativity inside the cells for distribution of ions, such as potassium, sodium, and chloride. Polarization is resting of the cardiac muscles cells, depolarization is charging and contracting of these cells, and repolarization is recovery of the cells.

99. Which cardiac arrhythmia is a contraction of the ventricles that occurs early?

A. Tachycardia
B. Bradycardia
C. Ectopic beat
D. Premature ventricular contraction

Answer: D. Premature ventricular contraction

Explanation: Bradycardia is a slow heartbeat (less than 60 beats per minute). Tachycardia is a fast heartbeat (more than 100 beats per minute). Asystole is absence of a heart rate (flat line). An ectopic beat is a beat that originates outside of the heart's pacemaker (SA node). A premature ventricular contraction (PVC) is a contraction of ventricles that occurs early. Ventricular fibrillation is uncoordinated ventricular contractions (quivering of the heart).Ventricular flutter is a ventricular rate of 150 to 300 beats per minute (considered life-threatening). A premature atrial contraction (PAC) is an atrial contraction that occurs early. Paroxysmal atrial tachycardia (PAT) is atrial tachycardia that occurs and subsides suddenly. Atrial fibrillation is an atrial rate of 350 to 500 beats per minute. Atrial flutter is an atrial rate of 250 to 350 beats per minute that produces a "saw tooth" pattern.

100. With right ventricular heart failure, which of the following would the EMT-B expect to see?

A. Jugular venous distension (JVD)
B. Chest pain
C. Pulmonary edema
D. Dyspnea

Answer: A. Jugular venous distension (JVD)

Explanation: With congestive heart failure, the ventricles are not able to adequately pump blood or handle the blood that is pumped into them. With right ventricular failure, the blood backs up into the venous system, causing jugular venous distension (JVD) and leg/foot swelling (edema). With left ventricular failure, the blood backs up into the lungs, causing pulmonary edema. Symptoms include dyspnea, chest pain, leg and foot swelling, and difficulty breathing lying down (orthopnea).

101. Of the following, which is NOT a usual cause of dehydration?

A. Chronic illness
B. Excessive perspiration
C. Diarrhea
D. Liver failure

Answer: D. Liver failure

Explanation: Homeostasis is the medical term that indicates relative stability of the internal body fluid balance. Fluid volume deficit is dehydration, which occurs when the fluid intake is not sufficient for the body. Dehydration is caused by inadequate fluid intake, fluid shifts between compartments, increased fluid loss from perspiration, diarrhea, and ketoacidosis, renal failure, chronic illness, and chronic malnutrition. Fluid volume deficit is corrected by administration of IV fluids, use of antidiarrheal medications, and treatment of the electrolyte imbalance, if necessary.

102. What is the goal of treatment for the patient with overhydration, who has taken in an excess volume of fluid?

A. To restore fluid and electrolyte balance.
B. To restore blood pressure.
C. To hydrate and stabilize.
D. All of the above

Answer: A. To restore fluid and electrolyte balance.

Explanation: Fluid volume excess occurs from overhydration, where fluid intake and retention exceeds the body's requirements. The goal of treatment is to correct electrolyte imbalances if present, eliminate the underlying cause of the overload, and restore fluid balance. Care interventions include stabilizing and monitoring for complications.

103. Which of the following measures is used to treat a patient with a cardiac emergency?

A. Nitroglycerine
B. Aspirin
C. Oxygen
D. All of the above

Answer: D. All of the above

Explanation: Any patient with chest pain or any cardiac emergency should be transported as high priority. The EMT-B should consider medications such as nitroglycerine and aspirin per standard EMS protocol and with approval of the medical director. Also, consider us of continuous positive airway pressure (CPAP) or bi-level positive airway pressure (BIPAP) for patients in heart failure.

104. When the EMS provider confirms a patient is experiencing cardiac compromise, he or she should administer oxygen through a nonrebreather mask at a rate of:

A. 2 liters per minute
B. 5 liters per minute
C. 10 liters per minute
D. 15 liters per minute

Answer: D. 15 liters per minute

Explanation: When the EMS provider confirms a patient is experiencing cardiac compromise, he or she should administer oxygen after placing the patient in a comfortable position. The oxygen can be given through a nonrebreather mask at a rate of 15 liters per minute.

105. After giving nitroglycerine to a patient with chest pain, the patient should be monitored for changes in blood pressure and LOC. If the patient experiences a systolic BP of less than 100, place him in:

A. Fowler's position
B. Semi-Fowler's position
C. Supine position
D. Trendelenburg position

Answer: D. Trendelenburg position

Explanation: After giving the nitroglycerine, the patient should be monitored for changes in blood pressure and LOC. If the patient experiences a systolic BP of less than 100, place him or her in the Trendelenburg position and reassess.

106. Defibrillation is used for emergency treatment for patients who are in:

A. Atrial fibrillation
B. Atrial flutter
C. Ventricular fibrillation
D. All of the above

Answer: C. Ventricular fibrillation

Explanation: Defibrillation is used for emergency treatment for patients who are in ventricular fibrillation, a form of irregular heartbeat. Also called v. flb, this arrhythmia is characterized by rapid electrical impulses. Defibrillation involves administering and electric shock to the heart with the purpose of reestablishing a normal rhythm. CPR is often performed along with defibrillation.

107. Which AED device is faster, and is usually preferred for treating emergency cardiac arrhythmias?

A. The semi-automatic automated external defibrillator (AED)
B. The fully automatic automated external defibrillator (AED)
C. The automated internal defibrillator (AID)
D. The automated internal defibrillator (AED)

Answer: B. The fully automatic automated external defibrillator (AED)

Explanation: The automated external defibrillator (AED) is a computer-controlled device that requires little manipulation for use. EMT-B providers can use the AED to administer life-saving treatment. The semi-automatic AED involves placement of patches and leads, so the user can analyze the rhythm. To administer a shock, only a push of a button is necessary. The fully automatic AED is quicker, and usually the preferred device.

108. When assessing a diabetic patient, the EMT-B finds that she has a finger-stick glucose of 42 mg/dL. What condition is this?

A. Hypoglycemia
B. Hyperglycemia
C. Normal
D. None of the above

Answer: A. Hypoglycemia

Explanation: A glucometer is used to assess capillary blood glucose levels. Normal readings are between 80 to 120 mg/dL, but less than 140 is considered normal after eating. Hypoglycemia is a reading of 60 or less, and hyperglycemia is when the level stays above 140 persistently.

109. The patient with hypoglycemia is at risk for which of the following complications:

A. Myocardial infarction
B. Hypothermia
C. Seizure
D. Syncope

Answer: C. Seizure

Explanation: Hypoglycemia is where the body's blood glucose levels are low, and this makes the patent appear intoxicated. Symptoms can be slurred speech, staggering, or unresponsiveness. If left untreated, hypoglycemia can result in seizures, coma, and even brain death.

110. A 72-year-old insulin-dependent diabetic patient has diaphoresis, tachycardia, and an altered LOC. His daughter reports that he took his insulin, but did not eat. What do you suspect?

A. Diabetic ketoacidosis
B. Insulin shock
C. Hyperglycemia
D. Hypoglycemia

Answer: B. Insulin shock

Explanation: Insulin shock is the medical term that refers to severe hypoglycemia with signs and symptoms. This is often caused when a patient take insulin and doesn't eat, or from excessive physical activity without adjustment of insulin or food intake. Symptoms of this include diaphoresis, tachycardia, cool and clammy skin, pallor, restlessness, and altered LOC.

111. The patient who has a blood glucose level of 210 mg/dL has:

A. Hypoglycemia
B. Hyperglycemia
C. Normal glucose
D. Diabetic ketoacidosis

Answer: B. Hyperglycemia

Explanation: Hyperglycemia is a sustained elevated blood glucose level, usually of 140 mg/dL or above. This causes the patient to have excessive thirst, dry mouth, thirst, and irritability. Hyperglycemia comes on slowly and is not dangerous unless glucose levels continue to rise.

112. You arrive on a scene and find a 33-year-old type 1 diabetic unresponsive. You notice that she has deep, long, and rapid breathing, as well as an unusual breath odor. What do you suspect?

A. Hypoglycemia
B. Hyperglycemia
C. Diabetic ketoacidosis
D. Insulin shock

Answer: C. Diabetic ketoacidosis

Explanation: More common for patients with type 1 diabetes, diabetic ketoacidosis (DKA) is when the glucose level goes above 350 mg/dL. The body will spill glucose into the urine and excrete it rapidly, which leads to dehydration. The symptoms and signs of DKA include Kussmaul respirations (deep, long, rapid breathing), the three Ps (polydipsia, polyphagia, and polyuria), unusual breath odor, tachycardia, and coma.

113. Which type of stroke is caused by bleeding within the brain itself, which affects oxygen flow and puts pressure on the brain tissue?

A. Hemorrhagic stroke
B. Ischemic stroke
C. Atypical stroke
D. Aneurysm

Answer: A. Hemorrhagic stroke

Explanation: A stroke is when there is death to the brain tissue from interruption in blood flow. Also called a cerebrovascular accident (CVA), current treatment for stroke can drastically result the amount of damage received form this condition. Ischemic strokes, the most common type, occur when there is blockage of blood flow to the brain, such as with atherosclerosis. Hemorrhagic strokes are caused by bleeding within the brain itself, and that bleeding affects oxygen flow and puts pressure on the brain tissue.

114. An 83-year-old woman has facial drooping, drooling, and slurred speech. When transferring her to the hospital, you also notice one-sided paralysis. What is this indicative of?

A. A brain aneurysm
B. A stroke
C. A myocardial infarction
D. None of the above

Answer: B. A stroke

Explanation: Signs and symptoms of a stroke include facial drooping and drooling, severe headache, slurred speech, one-sided (unilateral) numbness, weakness, and/or paralysis, altered LOC, visual disturbances, and trouble walking or moving.

115. What is the difference between a cerebrovascular accident (CVA) and a transient ischemic attack (TIA)?

A. The symptoms and signs of a TIA often resolve before 24 hours with no residual damage, whereas with a CVA that is not immediately treated, this is not the case.

B. The symptoms and signs of a CVA often resolve before 24 hours with no residual damage, whereas with a TIA that is not immediately treated, this is not the case.

C. The symptoms and signs of a TIA often resolve before 2 hours with no residual damage, whereas with a stroke that is not immediately treated, this is not the case.

D. The symptoms and signs of a CVA often resolve before 2 hours with no residual damage, whereas with a TIA that is not immediately treated, this is not the case.

Answer: A. The symptoms and signs of a TIA often resolve before 24 hours with no residual damage, whereas with a stroke that is not immediately treated, this is not the case.

Explanation: A transient ischemic attack (TIA) often has the same presentation as a CVA. However, the symptoms and signs often resolve before 24 hours with no residual damage. Also called mini strokes, a TIA is a warning sign of an impending stroke.

116. Also called a grand mal seizure, this type of seizure causes unresponsiveness and full body convulsions:

A. Absence seizure
B. Complex partial seizure
C. Partial seizure
D. Generalized seizure

Answer: D. Generalized seizure

Explanation: A seizure occurs when there is disorganized electrical activity of the brain. There are several types of seizures. These include generalized seizure, which is also called a grand mal seizure, and causes unresponsiveness and full body convulsions, absence seizure, which is also called petit mal seizure, and does not cause convulsions, and the patient does not interact with the environment, partial seizure, where there is no change in LOC, but the patient may have twitching and sensory changes, and complex partial seizure, which causes sensory changes, twitching, and altered LOC.

117. The medical term for passing out is:

A. Seizure
B. Syncope
C. Grand mal
D. Hypotension

Answer: B. Syncope

Explanation: Syncope is the medical term for passing out or fainting. This is caused form temporary loss of blood flow to the brain, as with hypotension, anemia, pregnancy, stress, a cardiac issue, or toxin exposure. Patients usually regain consciousness as soon as they are positioned in supine or Trendelenburg position.

118. Patients who experience a severe headache could have a/an:

A. Brain tumor
B. Aneurysm
C. Stroke
D. All of the above

Answer: D. All of the above

Explanation: A severe headache can occur from a stroke, hypertension, an aneurysm, a brain tumor, trauma, meningitis, or migraine. Symptoms vary according to headache cause, but often include head pain, elevated blood pressure, stiff neck, and neurological impairment.

119. For airway protection, seizure patients should be positioned in:

A. Semi-Fowler's position
B. Trendelenburg position
C. Lateral recumbent position
D. Supine position

Answer: C. Lateral recumbent position

Explanation: Seizure patients should be positioned in the lateral recumbent position for airway protection. If vomiting occurs, the long board must be tilted.

120. How can a patient come in contact with an antigen that could cause an allergic reaction?

A. Absorption
B. Ingestion
C. Inhalation
D. All of the above

Answer: D. All of the above

Explanation: When a patient comes in contact with a foreign substance (antigen), the immune system detects this and deploys antibodies to fight the antigens. This can be in the form of absorption, ingestion, injection, or inhalation.

121. A severe and life-threatening type of allergic reaction that causes impairment of the airway, respiratory system, and cardiovascular system is:

A. Anaphylaxis
B. Shock
C. Asthma
D. Hypersensitivity

Answer: A. Anaphylaxis

Explanation: Also known as anaphylactic shock, anaphylaxis is a severe and life-threatening type of allergic reaction. When this occurs, the patient has impairment of the airway, respiratory system, and cardiovascular system. Symptoms include airway swelling, increased mucus production, bronchoconstriction, hypotension, capillary leakage, flushed skin, hives, restlessness, irritability, dyspnea, wheezing, stridor, tachypnea, and hypotension.

122. A 17-year-old teen has hives, flushed skin, and dyspnea. When you are transporting him to the hospital, he reports that he recently took a new medication for an infection and also drank some orange juice. What do you suspect caused this?

A. The infection
B. The antibiotic
C. His age
D. The orange juice

Answer: B. The antibiotic

Explanation: Medications known to cause anaphylaxis include antibiotics, non-steroidal anti-inflammatory drugs (NSAIDs), aspirin, and even vitamins. Foods that many people are allergic to usually include peanuts, shellfish, and eggs, but other medicines and foods are known to cause allergic reactions.

123. A 22-year-old female has had a reaction to latex gloves she used when applying hair dye at home. She has severe dyspnea, wheezing, and a rash on both hands. What first line of treatment will the EMT-B give?

A. Nitroglycerine
B. Aspirin
C. Epinephrine
D. Atropine

Answer: C. Epinephrine

Explanation: Latex is a common allergen, and it is found in many medical supplies, including gloves. The first line of treatment for anaphylaxis is epinephrine, give per local protocol. Many patients often require oxygen administration, as well. When you assess the patient with allergic reaction, determine the exact cause and attempt to remove it from the situation.

124. A 55-year-old man who was gardening reports feeling a sharp pain at his ankle, and hearing something "move through the plants." He is experiencing tissue swelling, bruising, and petechia at the site. What could this indicate?

A. A nonpoisonous snake bite
B. A poisonous snake bite
C. An animal bite
D. A bee sting

Answer: B. A poisonous snake bite

Explanation: Poisonous snakebites can cause hemoptysis, hematuria, petechia, and extensive bruising from disseminated intravascular coagulation. A bite from a pit viper can cause tissue necrosis, massive tissue swelling, hypovolemic shock, and renal failure. A bite from a coral snake will cause mild, transient pain at the bite site, cranial and peripheral nerve defects, nausea, vomiting, and total flaccid paralysis.

125. When called to a scene where a patient has experienced a severe allergic reaction to a bee sting, what will the EMT-B most likely administer?

A. Intramuscular epinephrine
B. Intravenous fluids
C. Subcutaneous atropine
D. Oral antihistamine

Answer: A. Intramuscular epinephrine

Explanation: If a patient is allergic to bee stings, he or she will experience swelling at the sting site, wheezing, laryngeal edema, deterioration in mental status, and labored rapid breathing. Treatment for an anaphylactic reaction involves administration of 1.5 mL of 1:1000 epinephrine intramuscular. The patient also needs an intravenous line and cardiac monitoring. The EMS provider should instruct the patient to wear a medical alert bracelet, carry an EpiPen, and be cautious of areas where bees are likely to live.

126. You are called to a home where a 44 year old woman has ingested some mushrooms she picked out of the woods herself. She reports severe abdominal pain, cramping, and nausea. What could this indicate?

A. An allergic reaction
B. Acute gastroenteritis
C. Possible poisoning
D. Stomach virus

Answer: C. Possible poisoning

Explanation: Ingested toxins are consumed orally, such as cleaning products or mushrooms. These cause diarrhea, nausea, vomiting, abdominal pain, and cramps.

127. Absorption of a toxin can occur through the skin. This could occur from all of the following EXCEPT:

A. Dyes
B. Pesticides
C. Chemicals
D. Carbon monoxide

Answer: D. Carbon monoxide

Explanation: Absorbed toxins enter the body though the skin and cause itching, redness, burning, and swelling. Examples include dyes, pesticides, and chemicals. Carbon monoxide is an inhaled toxin.

128. Which type of abdominal pain is localized, severe, sharp, constant, and causes the patient to wince and appear uncomfortable?

A. Visceral
B. Parietal
C. Ischemic
D. Septic

Answer: B. Parietal

Explanation: Abdominal pain that is acute can occur from trauma, inflammation, distention, or ischemia. The types of abdominal pain are visceral and parietal. Visceral pain is dull and diffuse, difficult to localize, often associated with nausea and vomiting, and is often indicative of organ damage. Parietal pain is localized, severe, sharp, constant, and causes the patient to wince and appear uncomfortable.

129. Which type of abdominal pain occurs frequently in women who are aged 30 to 50 years, and is often in the right upper quadrant?

A. Appendicitis
B. Peritonitis
C. Cholecystitis
D. Diverticulitis

Answer: C. Cholecystitis

Explanation: Appendicitis, which is more common in young patients, is caused by an inflamed appendix, and it can lead to a life-threatening infection and septic shock. Most patients will complain of severe right lower quadrant abdominal pain. Peritonitis is the result of an inflamed peritoneum, which is the membrane lining the abdominal organs and cavity. Most patients will present with nausea, vomiting, diarrhea, and fever. Cholecystitis is gall bladder inflammation, which can be the result of gallstones. It often occurs in women age 30 to 50 years, and leads to upper right quadrant pain, nausea, vomiting, and referred discomfort to the shoulder. With diverticulitis, there are inflamed and infected diverticula (small pouches of the intestines). This mostly affects older people, and leads to weakness, lower abdominal pain, fever, nausea, and vomiting.

130. All of the following are symptoms and signs of GI bleeding EXCEPT:

A. Vomiting blood
B. Blood in the stool
C. Hypovolemia
D. Hypertension

Answer: D. Hypertension

Explanation: GI bleeding occurs in middle-aged persons, and can be fatal for many geriatric persons. Most upper GI bleeding is due to ulcers, whereas lower GI bleeding occurs from diverticulitis. Symptoms include vomiting blood, blood in the stool, and hypovolemic shock with excessive blood loss.

131. Which patient population is at the highest risk for an abdominal aortic aneurysm?

A. Young women age 20 to 40 years
B. Young men age 25 to 45 years
C. Middle aged women
D. Geriatric men

Answer: D. Geriatric men

Explanation: When the wall of the aorta in the abdomen weakens, an abdominal aortic aneurysm (AAA) can develop. This is often common in geriatric men, and a ruptured AAA is often fatal due to massive blood loss. The symptoms include tearing back pain, pulsating abdominal mass, and hypovolemic shock.

132. A patient with a kidney stone will often complain of which of the following group of symptoms?

A. Leg pain, burning with urination, and hiccups
B. Groin discomfort, nausea, and painful urination
C. Chest pain, blood in the urine, and headaches
D. All of the above

Answer: B. Groin discomfort, nausea, and painful urination

Explanation: Renal calculi (kidney stones) occur when crystals form in the kidneys and cause obstruction. Men have kidney stones more frequently, and they lead to severe abdominal and back pain, groin discomfort, painful urination, nausea, vomiting, and fever.

133. Certain patients with abdominal pain are considered high-risk. Of the following, which would NOT be concerning?

A. A 64-year-old woman with bleeding and vomiting.
B. A 52-year-old man with chronic low back pain.
C. A 27-year-old man with severe back and flank pain.
D. A 74-year-old woman with diabetes.

Answer: B. A 52-year-old-man with chronic low back pain.

Explanation: The EMS provider should be cautious with patients who complain of abdominal pain. Patients at risk for various serious conditions include women of child-bearing age who have acute abdominal pain; any person with bleeding, vomiting, syncope, trauma, or signs of shock; patients who have severe back or flank pain; and geriatric and diabetic patients.

134. Which mechanism of heat loss occurs from direct transfer of heat through contact with a cold surface?

A. Conduction
B. Radiation
C. Convection
D. Respiration

Answer: A. Conduction

Explanation: The body loses heat by five basic mechanisms: conduction, which is direct transfer of heat through contact with a cold surface, such as the floor or ground, convection, which is loss of heat to passing air, such as a cold breeze, evaporation, which is loss of heat through water evaporation through the skin, such as getting out of a warm pool or shower, respiration, where exhaled air is warmed within the body in a cold environment, but that heat is lost with exhalation, and radiation, which is direct transfer of radiant hat, as with walking into a freezer.

135. Which type of hypothermia affects the entire body?

A. Frostnip
B. Frostbite
C. Generalized hypothermia
D. Localized hypothermia

Answer: C. Generalized hypothermia

Explanation: Hypothermia is a condition where there is excessive exposure to cold climates, and the body temperature falls well below 98.6 degrees F. Generalized hypothermia affects the entire body, with the main signs being altered mental status and impaired motor function. The body attempts to raise the temperature by elevating both heart and respiratory rates.

136. Of the following, which is NOT a typical sign or symptom of hypothermia?

A. Altered LOC
B. Trouble speaking
C. Pale or cyanotic skin
D. Nausea and/or vomiting

Answer: D. Nausea and/or vomiting

Explanation: The signs and symptoms of hypothermia include pale or cyanotic skin, shivering, stiff muscles, difficulty speaking, and altered LOC. The patient may have hypotension, bradycardia, and bradypnea, as well.

137. A dangerous local cold emergency where the tissue becomes frozen, which often leads to permanent damage (gangrene) is:

A. Frostnip
B. Frostbite
C. Hypothermia
D. Hyperthermia

Answer: B. Frostbite

Explanation: Frostnip develops when certain parts of the body get extremely cold, but are not yet frozen. Also called chilblains, frostnip symptoms and signs include pale, cold skin and loss of sensation in affected area. Frostbite is a dangerous local cold emergency where the tissue becomes frozen, and this often leads to permanent damage (gangrene).

138. Which of the following symptoms would you expect to see with frostbite, but not frostnip?

A. Blistering of the skin
B. Pale skin
C. Cyanotic skin
D. Loss of sensation to the area

Answer: A. Blistering of the skin

Explanation: The signs and symptoms of frostbite include hard, frozen body tissue, possible mottling, and occasional blistering. Frostnip symptoms and signs include pale, cold skin and loss of sensation in affected area, but not blistering.

139. What is a contributing factor to hyperthermia?

A. Hypotension
B. Hypertension
C. Dehydration
D. Overhydration

Answer: C. Dehydration

Explanation: Hyperthermia occurs when a patient's body temperature rises and is sustained well above 98.6 degrees F. This is most common in humid, hot weather, and dehydration is a contributing factor for hyperthermia. The symptoms of this condition include dizziness, weakness, muscle cramps, rapid heartbeat, nausea, vomiting, and altered mental status.

140. First aid measures for heat stroke include all of the following EXCEPT:

A. Wetting the patient with icy water.
B. Placing ice packs on the neck, chest, axillae, and groin.
C. Removing excessive clothes.
D. Using tepid water to sponge down the patient.

Answer: A. Wetting the patient with icy water.

Explanation: First aid measures for heat stroke include placing ice on the neck, chest, axillae, and groin, removing clothes, and wetting the patient with tepid water. Older adults are at increased risk for heat-related illnesses.

141. A 24 year old man is having tachycardia and reports dizziness, weakness, and muscle cramps. He has been at the beach for over six hours, and reports surfing the entire time and only took in one soda. What does this indicate?

A. Heat exhaustion
B. Heat stroke
C. Hyperthermia
D. Heat emergency

Answer: A. Heat exhaustion

Explanation: One systemic heat emergency that occurs occasionally is heat exhalation, which is caused by hypovolemia and heat exposure. The signs and symptoms of this condition include dizziness, weakness, tachycardia, headache, thirst, muscle cramps, nausea, and vomiting.

142. Predisposing factors for heat stroke include all of the following EXCEPT:

A. High humidity
B. Obesity
C. Dehydration
D. Diabetes

Answer: D. Diabetes

Explanation: Predisposing factors include high humidity, obesity, seizures, dehydration, and use of beta-adrenergic blockers.

143. You are called out to a scene where a victim was waterskiing and hit her head. She was rendered unconscious and has shallow respirations. For this near-drowning victim, what is the first measure to take?

A. Remove fluid from the airway.
B. Give artificial ventilation
C. Give epinephrine
D. Cover with a blanket

Answer: A. Remove fluid from the airway

Explanation: Near-drowning incidents can occur when a victim strikes an object while engaging in water sports, such as skiing or swimming. This is when a patient survives an immersion event. These injuries usually involve spinal trauma, so the patient should be immobilized. A near-drowning victim will require fluid removal from the airway, and artificial ventilation is used during transport.

144. How many back blows should the EMT-B administer between the shoulders of an infant, when attempting to remove an object from the airway?

A. 2
B. 3
C. 4
D. 5

Answer: D. 5

Explanation: To remove an obstruction in an infant, position the infant so he or she is face down and deliver five back blows between the shoulders. Turn the infant face up and assess for the object. If not seen, deliver five chest thrust over the lower half of the sternum. Repeat this until the airway is unobstructed or the child becomes responsive.

145. In pediatric patients, an altered mental status can occur from all of the following EXCEPT:

A. Hypoglycemia
B. Hypoperfusion
C. Head trauma
D. Dehydration

Answer: D. Dehydration

Explanation: In pediatric patients, an altered mental status can occur from poisoning, head trauma, infection, hypoglycemia, infection, head trauma, hypoperfusion, and decreased oxygen levels.

146. When doing the pediatric assessment triangle, which includes assessment of appearance, what does TICLS mean?

A. Time, Interaction, Convection, Limp, and Sound
B. Tone, Interactivity, Consolability, Look, and Speech
C. Tension, Inspiration, Congestion, Listen, and Speak
D. Treat, Interact, Console, Listen, and Suction

Answer: B. Tone, Interactivity, Consolability, Look, and Speech

Explanation: The pediatric assessment triangle (PAT) includes appearance, breathing, and circulation. Appearance involves: Tone, Interactivity, Consolability, Look, and Speech (TICLS).

147. Which ambulance type has a truck chassis with modular ambulance body?

A. Type I
B. Type II
C. Type III
D. Type IV

Answer: A. Type I

Explanation: Type I – Truck chassis with modular ambulance body. Type II – Standard van design. Type III ambulance – Specialty van design with a square patient compartment mounted on the chassis.

148. When an air ambulance is on the ground, the EMT-B should approach it from:

A. The side
B. The front
C. The back
D. Any of the above

Answer: B. The front

Explanation: Never approach the air ambulance without permission, and always approach from the front. Make sure that all loose items are secured before attempting to approach the aircraft to load the patient. Be familiar with local protocols that are related to air medical operations. Not all patients should be transferred via the air route.

149. The term for the process where the patient is removed from the vehicle or any other dangerous situation is:

A. Extraction
B. Extrication
C. Evacuation
D. Elevation

Answer: B. Extrication

Explanation: Extrication is the term for the process where the patient is removed from the vehicle or any other dangerous situation. In many incidences, you must remove objects and debris from the area first, which is called disentanglement. Specialized equipment may be necessary for this process.

150. You are called out to a scene where there has been a hazardous material spill. The first measure when approaching the scene is:

A. To remove all bystanders and victims.
B. To isolate and avoid the area where the hazardous material is located.
C. To clean up the hazardous material.
D. To label all areas.

Answer: B. To isolate and avoid the area where the hazardous material is located.

Explanation: The first measure when approaching the scene is to isolate and avoid the area where the hazardous material is located. This involves recognizes sounds, clouds, or odors that indicate the presence of hazardous materials. When doing this, it is vital that you report anything unusual to dispatch.

151. The U.S. Department of Labor requires organizations to keep these as public records for all chemicals used:

A. Material Security Diagnosis Sheets
B. Material Safety Data Sheets
C. Multiple Substance Data Signs
D. Multiple Substance Diagnosis Sheets

Answer: B. Material Safety Data Sheets

Explanation: Material Safety Data Sheets (MSDS) are electronic or hard copy papers that explain detains about the substance or chemical. The U.S. Department of Labor requires organizations to keep these as public records for all chemicals used. This information will help EMS providers to deal with hazardous materials. Place the material in a container when found, making sure it is noted if the chemical is flammable, radioactive, or corrosive.

152. Incident management systems are used for:

A. Hazardous material scenes
B. Multiple extrication incidents
C. Helping crewmembers understand their responsibilities.
D. All of the above

Answer: All of the above

Explanation: Local and state organizations create incident management systems to ensure efficient and effective responses by police and fire departments, as well as EMS crews. These systems will help the crew members understand their responsibilities. These systems are used in situations involving multiple extrications or hazardous materials.

153. This chemical weapon of mass destruction can lead to blistering, pain, and burns to the skin, respiratory tract, and eyes:

A. Nerve agent
B. Vesicant
C. Cyanide
D. Pulmonary agent

Answer: B. Vesicant

Explanation: Nerve agents are a significant threat due to their ease of use and how easily they are acquired. These agents cause excessive parasympathetic nervous system stimulation. Vesicants can lead to blistering, pain, and burns to the skin, respiratory tract, and eyes. Also called blistering agents, these agents have a delayed onset of action, and affected areas should be irrigated with large amounts of water as soon as exposure occurs. Cyanide is a substance that interferes with the body's ability to deliver oxygen to the cells, and this often leads to hypoxia and death. Known as a blood agent, cyanide symptoms and signs include weakness, dizziness, anxiety, tachypnea, nausea, seizures, and respiratory arrest. Also referred to as choking agents, pulmonary agents cause lung damage. The symptoms and signs of these include dyspnea, wheezing, runny nose, cough, and sore throat. Management of these agents includes maintaining the airway, giving the patient oxygen as needed, and ventilation support.

154. The structure that delivers air from the larynx to the lungs is referred to as:

A. Trachea
B. Bronchus
C. Epiglottis
D. Pharynx

Answer: A. Trachea

Explanation: The trachea is the tube that runs from the oropharyngeal area to where it branches into the two bronchi, and they deliver air on into the lungs